80
DAYS

80 DAYS THAT CHANGED THE WORLD

For TIME Weekly
Managing Editor: James Kelly
Deputy Managing Editor: Stephen Koepp
News Director: Howard Chua-Eoan
Assistant Managing Editor: Janice C. Simpson
Editor-at-Large: Bill Saporito
Art Director: Arthur Hochstein
Picture Editor: Michele Stephenson
Chief of Reporters: Jane Bachman Wulf
Director, Research Center: Jim Oberman
Senior Writer: Richard Corliss
Staff Writer: James Poniewozik
Art Director, TIME Canada: Edel Rodriguez

Associate Picture Editor: Robert B. Stevens
Associate Art Director: Christine Dunleavy
Senior Reporter: Barbara Maddux
Reporters: Mitch Frank, Deirdre van Dyk

For Time Inc. Home Entertainment
Editor: Kelly Knauer
Design: Ellen Fanning
Picture Editor: Patricia Cadley
Copy Editor: Bruce Christopher Carr
Research: Matthew M. Fenton
Production Editor: Michael Skinner
Research Associate: Rudi Papiri

TIME INC.
HOME ENTERTAINMENT

President
Rob Gursha

Vice President, Branded Businesses
David Arfine

Vice President, New Product Development
Richard Fraiman

Executive Director, Marketing Services
Carol Pittard

Director, Retail & Special Sales
Tom Mifsud

Director of Finance
Tricia Griffin

Assistant Marketing Director
Ann Marie Doherty

Prepress Manager
Emily Rabin

Book Production Manager
Jonathan Polsky

Assistant Product Manager
Sara Stumpf

Special thanks to: Bozena Bannett, Robert Dente, Gina Di Meglio, Anne-Michelle Gallero, Peter Harper, Suzanne Janso, Robert Marasco, Natalie McCrea, Mary Jane Rigoroso, Steven Sandonato, Lamarr Tsufura

THE EDITORS OF TIME PRESENT

80 DAYS

THAT CHANGED THE WORLD

CONTENTS

AUG. 28, 1963: With his vision of a united America, Rev. Martin Luther King "subpoenaed the conscience of the nation"

Why History Doesn't Follow the Rules

The world can change in a day, all right, but not always the way we think it will

By Jeff Greenfield

APW/WIDE WORLD

L ooking for a lesson in humility? Stand at a major historical marker, and try drawing a perfectly reasonable, prudent conclusion about where that marker is pointing. Believe me, if you read about a 15th century traveler saying, "I have to get back to Italy now; the Renaissance is starting," you're reading a line from a Woody Allen story. Real life rarely offers such prescience, even from the people paid to deliver it. Some of the days commemorated in this 80-year retrospective slipped by unnoticed at the time. Who could imagine that a gizmo to help techno-nerds talk to one another with their computers would so radically alter how we all would connect with one another? Other days might not have made the list at all if it had been put together a decade ago. History comes with its very own Doppler effect: as our point of observation changes, so does our understanding of what we are seeing.

Think back to July 20, 1969. If you were watching when Neil Armstrong set foot on the moon, you almost certainly believed that this "one small step" was the first in an imminent journey out to the planets and the stars. A year earlier, Stanley Kubrick's *2001: A Space Odyssey* had portrayed a near future where Pan Am spaceships carried business travelers and va-

July 20, 1969

DAWN? No. The Apollo program proved a dead end

cationers to the moon. Who would have believed then that when 2001 rolled around, there would be no trips to the moon—and for that matter, no Pan Am.

Look at what we all "knew" on that August day in 1974 when Richard Nixon waved goodbye, boarded a helicopter and flew off into exile. The scandal that engulfed Nixon, his first Vice President, Attorney General and top White House aides was, nearly everyone agreed, clearly a windfall of immense proportions for the Democratic Party. And it was: in the 1974 midterm elections that gave the Democrats huge Congressional gains—43 House seats and three Senate seats—and in the unlikely elevation of a peanut farmer and Washington outsider named Jimmy Carter to the presidency two years later. In the long term, however, Watergate proved to be more of a boon for Republicans as it helped convince Americans of a bedrock conservative tenet: government is not to be trusted, the people in power in Washington are up to no good. When President Reagan told us in his 1981 Inaugural Address that "government is not the solution to our problem; government is the problem," it was the memory of Watergate that had many in his audience saying "Amen."

Or look at what happened after the Ayatullah Khomeini seized power in Iran in 1979 and raised the specter of a radical, anti-American Islamic nation with messianic impulses for the region. Over the next decade two Presidents, anxious for a counterforce to Iran's fundamentalist ambitions, gave diplomatic, financial and military assistance to the secular, "modernist" regime of Iraq's Saddam Hussein. By 1990, with Saddam in Kuwait and threatening the Saudis, the U.S. realized the error of its ways and dispatched half a million troops to help free Kuwait from the grip of its neighbor Iraq. Surely, we assumed, the response among Muslims would be one of gratitude. Instead we got Osama bin Laden's homicidal fury at the "desecration" of the holy lands by "infidels" that has led to escalating terror against all things Western.

The creation of Israel in 1948 and the fall of the Iron Cur-

Feb. 1, 1979

BETTMANN CORBIS

ENEMY? Yes, but Khomeini drove the U.S. to embrace Saddam

tain early in the 1990s also seemed as though they would mark the end of old enmities, only to set the stage for more than five decades of strife between Jews and Arabs in that Holy Land and the recent bloody wars in the Balkan states. And who predicted, when the Soviet invasion of Afghanistan turned into Moscow's Vietnam, that freedom fighters who had triumphed with the aid of U.S.-supplied Stinger missiles would just a few years later morph into the Taliban and turn that nation into a haven and staging area for al-Qaeda?

Of course, revised views of history are what keeps successive generations of historians in business, continuously updating where the latest dominoes have fallen. Eighty years from now, scholars will still be debating the meaning of what happened 80—or even 800—years ago. We journalists like to say that journalism is the first rough draft of history—a rare acknowledgment, perhaps, that there is a Higher Authority in whose hands rests the final draft. ∎

Jeff Greenfield is CNN's senior analyst and a contributor to Inside Politics with Judy Woodruff.

Aug. 9, 1974

DOWNFALL? Yes, but Nixon's deeds gave the G.O.P, not the Democrats, a long-term boost

Nov. 9, 1989

TRIUMPH? Yes, but the power vacuum after the Wall's fall bred monsters

In an accelerated period of exuberant energy,
radio was the rage; Duke Ellington and Louis
Armstrong set the tempo; and Jack Dempsey,
Babe Ruth and Red Grange thrilled sports fans.
Prohibition—intended to calm America
down—only helped jazz up the Jazz Age

1920s

DEC. 27, 1927 Unflinching in its portrayal of America's complex racial heritage, *Show Boat,* by Jerome Kern and Oscar Hammerstein, freed musical comedy to explore serious issues

DEC. 4, 1927 Duke Ellington began a three-year run at the Cotton Club, where scantily clad dancers sashayed and swung

SEPT. 22, 1927 Jack Dempsey sends Gene Tunney reeling in the seventh round of their great rematch for the heavyweight crown. But a long count gave Tunney a second chance—and ultimately victory

Oct. 29, 1923

Atatürk Commands His People: Westward, Ho!

General Mustafa Kemal, who had repelled the British at Gallipoli in 1915 and had just recently done the same to invading Greeks, now planned a civil take-over of his own country. Just hours before he did it, Kemal was telling a journalist that popular Islam had become a morass of superstitions that would destroy those who professed it. He declared, "We will save them," accord-ing to biographer Andrew Mango. A 101-gun salute greeted the announcement: Turkey had ceased to be an Islamic em-pire. It was a republic, and its leader, Kemal, became Presi-dent—not Sultan, not Caliph, the titles that Ottoman monarchs paraded for 600 years, the first as despots who once made Eu-rope cower, the second as "Commanders of the Faithful," leaders of Sunni Muslims everywhere. Soon Western cloth-

ERDOGAN:
Will Turkey's
new boss roll
back Atatürk's
grand plan?

■ A Land Still Divided

Eighty years after Mustafa Kemal Atatürk revolutionized his nation and turned its face toward Europe, Turkey remains an outsider in two worlds, held at arm's length by both its European and Arab neighbors. Long a member of NATO, Atatürk's nation smarted as the European Union accepted a gaggle of former Warsaw Pact nations but put Turkey on hold. On Istanbul's streets, conservative Muslims pass artsy young women with their hair uncovered. In its governing councils, democracy and its freedoms are hailed as shining ideals, but open debate is discouraged. In some ways, the nation is not so far removed from the days of Atatürk, a dictator-of-democracy who issued fiats banning Arab garb—in the name of freedom.

Turkey's ruling élites followed Atatürk's resolute secularism for decades, but lately some Turks have called for a society more in tune with the nation's Islamic heritage. In the November 2002 elections, voters threw out the longtime ruling party in favor of a pro-Islamic party headed by former Istanbul Mayor Recep Tayyip Erdogan. Turkey soon found itself caught between its twin beacons: U.S. President George W. Bush wanted Turkey to allow U.S. troops to invade Iraq from Turkish soil, but in a major blow to U.S. plans, the new Parliament vetoed the plan. With the U.S. looking forward to a post-Saddam Middle East, its diplomats will confront a Turkey in evolution, as the most democratic nation in the Islamic world turns its face toward Mecca again.

ing was enforced and Roman letters replaced Arabic-based script. The man who would adopt the name Atatürk ("father of the Turks") inaugurated an era in which nationalism, not Islam, would be seen as the solution to the troubles of Muslim peoples. But by the 1980s, a reaction would set in, and the cause of the caliphate eventually would be taken up by, among others, Osama bin Laden. —*By Howard Chua-Eoan*

Mustapha Kemal Pasha ... has lifted the people out of the slough of servile submission to alien authority, brought them to ... independence of thought and action.
— *March 24, 1923*

FREE TIME: Hitler's prison stay was far from punitive. Hess is second from right

THE FUTURE FÜHRER
Hitler with supporters during the abortive putsch

■ Out of Harm's Way?

While supposedly locked safely away from society in prison, Adolf Hitler created the work that would carry his message into millions of German hearts and minds. Removed from day-to-day political organizing, the jailed agitator now paused to collect his thoughts—if not exactly to organize them—and to concoct the engine that would drive his rise to power.

During the eight months he spent in Munich's Landsberg Prison, Hitler wrote his autobiography. Taking the advice of Max Amann, his political and business ally and former company commander in World War I, he dictated his rambling theories on race, power, propaganda and German identity to his close associate and fellow prisoner Rudolf Hess and his chauffeur, Emil Maurice. The result was *Mein Kampf* (My Struggle), a shortened version of a more pungent original title, *A Four-and-a-Half-Year Struggle Against Lies, Stupidity and Cowardice*. The first print run, in 1925, was 10,000 copies.

Eight years later, *Mein Kampf* was the Nazi bible, 8 million copies of what the New York *Times* called "a hymn of hate" were in print in Germany, and Adolf Hitler was Chancellor of the Reich.

What TIME Said Then

The door opened and in walked Herr Hitler ... with some of [his] followers, who fired a few shots into the ceiling by way of effect. Herr Hitler ... elected himself not only head of Bavaria but Chancellor of all Germany ... There was wild talk of a march on Berlin ...
—Nov. 19, 1923

Adolf Hitler's Practice Power Grab

Nov. 8, 1923

The man with the square moustache jumped onto a table and fired a shot into the ceiling of the Buerger-bräukeller, a large beer hall in Munich. "The national revolution has begun," he shouted. Not quite. Adolf Hitler was forcing the issue. With Germany seething at the spineless Weimar government over the humiliating terms of the World War I armistice, Hitler sensed an opportunity. Just before 9 p.m., his Nazis launched a putsch, or *coup d'état*, taking three powerful officials hostage. With hundreds of his Storm Troopers surrounding the hall, he compelled the trio to support him. But Nazi euphoria was fleeting; Hitler's three "supporters" slipped away and denounced him. Police opened fire on the Nazis when they took to the streets the next day. Hitler was arrested. The putsch was a joke. But at his trial, Hitler beguiled the populace with orations for restoring German greatness. After serving only eight months of a five-year sentence, he emerged from jail with the first part of his seminal work of Nazism, *Mein Kampf*. The joke would have a devastating punch line.

—By Howard Chua-Eoan

Jan. 21, 1924

An Old Bolshevik's Troubled Legacy

Vladimir Ilich Ulyanov, who used some 160 pseudonyms, the most famous being Lenin, woke up at 10:30 a.m. on the day he was to die. About 18 months earlier, he had suffered a massive stroke and never fully recovered, so 10:30 was not so late for the old revolutionary to rise. He had some coffee, but it did not take, and he went back to bed. By evening Lenin was running a high fever, as Oxford historian Robert Service recounts in *Lenin: A Biography*. Lenin's Bolshevik buddy Nikolai Bukharin was there at the end: "When I ran into Ilich's room, full of doctors and stacked with medicines, Ilich let out a last sigh ... Ilich, Ilich was no more."

The cause of death remains uncertain—some say it was syphilis; others say an operation to remove a bullet from his neck damaged him. (He had been shot in 1918 by a young anarchist who was herself promptly shot.) One theory among good communists was that Lenin, who was just 53, had simply worked himself to death; he had driven himself hard, especially for a son of such a prosperous family. (One of his grandfathers had been a landowner who personally controlled over 40 peasant families.)

Lenin's early death opened the way for the horrors of Stalin. Would Lenin have stopped them? The latest scholarship reminds us that Leninism was a brutal philosophy. As historian Hélène d'Encausse wrote in her 2001 biography, "On the threshold of death, Lenin had hardly changed": he never backed away from the one-party, one-ideology, resolutely self-protecting state. When asked once why a group of political foes needed killing, Lenin had replied, "Don't you understand that if we do not shoot these few leaders we may be placed in a position where we would need to shoot 10,000 workers?" But Stalin would turn out to be a man with not one qualm about murdering 10,000—or 10 million. Lenin had criticized Stalin, who had become General Secretary in 1922, for "concentrat[ing] unlimited power in his hands." He had no idea just how much power Comrade Stalin would wield after that January eve. **—By John Cloud**

R.I.P.? Over his widow's protests, Lenin was embalmed and put on display. Thus he has outlasted the U.S.S.R.

What TIME Said Then

Stalin, Stalin, Stalin. Nothing so disagrees as prophecy, yet there has been scarcely a comment as to Russia's future that has not mentioned Stalin, Commisar of Police. It is an assumed name—a derivative from the Russian word for "steel." —*Feb. 4, 1924*

The 40-Hour Revolution

No industrialist enjoyed upsetting the apple cart more than Henry Ford. In 1914 he announced that he would pay $5 a day to his workers, double the going rate. With the extra cash, Ford reasoned, they could purchase his Model Ts. The workers were becoming a bulwark of the middle class.

Ford's next act came in September 1926, when he pioneered the five-day workweek. As he noted in his company's *Ford News*, "Just as the eight-hour day opened our way to prosperity in America, so the five-day workweek will open our way to still greater prosperity ... It is high time to rid ourselves of the notion that leisure for workmen is either lost time or a class privilege."

The five-day week, Ford figured, would encourage industrial workers to vacation and shop on Saturday. Soon, manufacturers all over the world followed his lead. "People who have more leisure must have more clothes," he argued. "They eat a greater variety of food. They require more transportation in vehicles." Taking advantage of his own wisdom, he discontinued the Model T and then, on a Saturday, launched the Model A. The 1927 unveiling would see 10,534,992 people visiting dealerships just to glimpse the latest product of the Sage of Dearborn. — **By Douglas Brinkley**

Brinkley wrote the forthcoming Wheels for the World: Henry Ford, His Company, and a Century of Progress 1903-2003

WEEKDAYS Men on the assembly line at a Ford factory in Chicago in 1926

Sept. 25, 1926

D.20

ICARUS DESCENDING:
Lindbergh at an airplane
factory in Bremen, 1936

May. 21, 1927

AP/WIDE WORLD

TOUCHDOWN:
*The Spirit of St.
Louis* is engulfed
by well-wishers

AP/WIDE WORLD

■ The Glare of Publicity

Charles Lindbergh was one of the most lionized Americans in history. His 1927 flight coincided with an explosive period of media growth, fueled by new technology, that put the roar in the Roaring Twenties. Within a few months of his flight, he was probably the most famous man on earth, his feat amplified by a host of new voices. Earlier American heroes had been celebrated in newspapers; Lindbergh could be seen in the popular new newsreels at the movies; could be discussed on the burgeoning radio networks; could be read about in smart new magazines like the *New Yorker* and TIME, which named him its first Man of the Year.

Lindbergh soon fell victim to his own celebrity. The 1932 kidnapping of his son became a frightful media circus; the Lindberghs escaped by taking up residence in England. Yet even though he knew his every move was under intense scrutiny, Lindbergh made six visits to Hitler's Germany between 1936 and 1939. After he accepted a medal from Luftwaffe commander Hermann Göring, many Americans began to question—or condemn—his judgment.

What TIME Said Then

His first words were "Well, here we are. I am very happy…" Some of the crowd of 25,000 attempted to strip souvenirs from the *Spirit of St. Louis*, while the majority escorted Captain Lindbergh, on somebody's shoulders, to a nearby clubhouse. —*May 30, 1927*

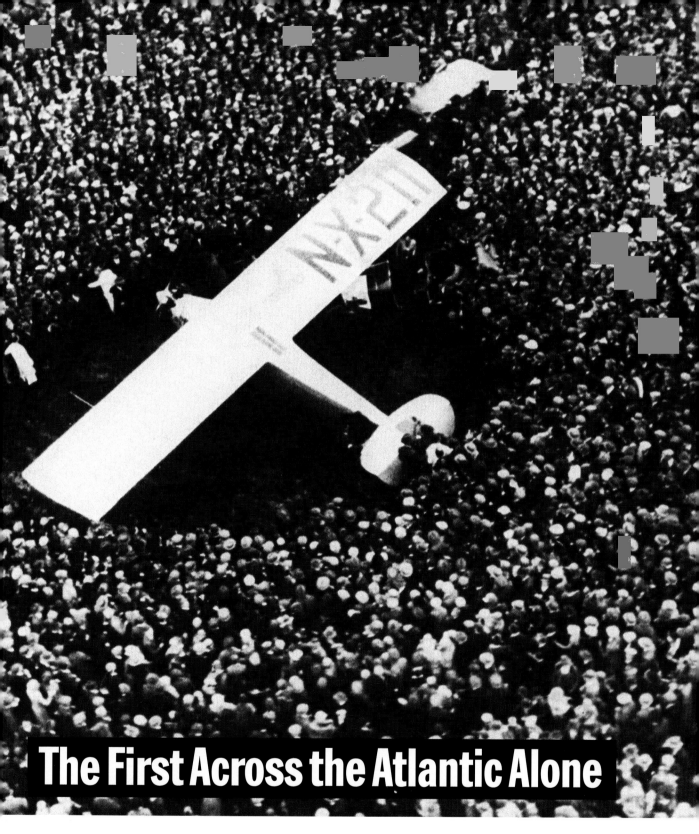

The First Across the Atlantic Alone

The $25,000 prize was beside the point, especially when ice on a wing or sleep could be fatal. Charles Lindbergh had flown the *Spirit of St. Louis* from California to New York, so he was used to the air-cooled Whirlwind engine, a splendid name for something attached to little more than a flying gasoline can. But the Atlantic was ocean, with no chance of a soft landing for 4,000 miles. He crossed it in 33½ hours, the first to do it solo and nonstop.

You'd think he'd brag. But Anne Morrow, who married him, recalled being captivated by his shyness. It burnished her image of his landing at Le Bourget airfield, "the picture of that mad crowd, that whole nation surging around his plane in Paris," she wrote. "I can see how they all worship him … His glance [was] keener, clearer and brighter than anyone else's, lit with a more intense fire." He was, she said, one of the "great bulldozers" of the century. —*By Howard Chua-Eoan*

Oct. 6, 1927

When Pictures Began to Talk

Wait a minute, wait a minute! You ain't heard nothin' yet!" cried Al Jolson halfway through *The Jazz Singer.* Jolson's urgent, boastful bray—an ad-libbed intro to his rendition of *Toot Toot Tootsie*—cut through the opening-night audience at the Warner Theatre near Times Square like an obstetrician's scissors severing the umbilical cord to silent films, for 30 years the dominant screen language. But the movies had to talk. Thomas Edison thought so. He and his assistant W.K.L. Dickson had devised a talking-movie machine as early as 1889. In the early '20s short sound films appeared featuring vaudeville and opera stars. These were sensible, tentative steps; now

the maverick Warner brothers made a great leap of faith. Their *Jazz Singer* wasn't a true "talkie"; it broke free from silent-screen traditions only for brief dialogue and a few songs. Nor was the story, about a cantor's son who goes into show business, at all modern. But Jolson's hip-swiveling salesmanship (he was in many ways the Elvis of his day) put over the novelty of talking pictures.

The film, an immediate sensation, cued a frantic rush to convert all studios and movie theaters to sound, and signaled the end of a pristine, vigorous silent-film art. By 1930 almost every U.S. film was a talkie, and movies haven't shut up since. Jolson's slangy cry was truly the shout heard 'round the world.

—By Richard Corliss

MAMMY! Jolson sings to Eugenie Besserer, and for the first time the world can listen

What TIME Said Then

[Jolson] is a good actor; but he is a very great singer of popular songs. In cities where the Vitaphone can be installed and reproduce his voice this picture will eminently repay attendance.
— *Oct. 17, 1927*

The Mouse That Roared

In the fall of 1928, Walt Disney could claim three dubious assets: a new animated cartoon character called Mickey Mouse, three short silent films featuring the spunky rodent and an idea greater than perhaps even he imagined—adding sound tracks to his little films.

What he didn't have as he wandered New York City with one of those films, *Steamboat Willie*, tucked under his arm was cash or clout. He was just an unknown 27-year-old animator from California who needed musicians and sound-effects guys to record a score—and a distributor to promote his product.

It was seemingly an impossible dream. A year earlier Warner Bros. had released the first (partial) talkie, *The Jazz Singer*, and the movie biz was in a tizzy. The Al Jolson movie was awful, but the man sang and spoke. A long-sought miracle had arrived. Unfortunately, the camera, heavily blimped to prevent its whirrings from being recorded, was immobilized. Now that movies could finally talk, they could no longer move gracefully.

That's where Disney came in. His animators' drawn images were as free as any in movie history. It was relatively easy to pre-plan music, effects and dialogue so that they could be synched to the imagery. For example, all a conductor had to do was follow the beats that Disney's people had marked on their work print. Even so, Disney had to spend a good deal of his dwindling capital getting a musical director to follow those cues. Then he had to spend several weeks lurking around screening rooms, trying to get Willie seen and heard by the men with the money.

To no avail. At which point enters legendary press agent Harry Reichenbach, master of old-fashioned ballyhoo (he had once faked a star's kidnapping to promote a film). Reichenbach was managing the Colony Theater in New York City, and he advised Disney to appeal directly to the public. Give me your little movie for a two-week run, he told Disney, and I'll give you $1,000 and make your mouse famous. The producer was dubious but desperate to make payroll—and he made the deal.

And so, on Nov. 18, history happened. There were bigger stars on the Colony's stage and screen, but Steamboat Willie got the press. Crowds created near mob scenes as they rushed to see this "riot of mirth." In truth, it was crude stuff. But Mickey turned a cow's tail into a hurdy-gurdy handle, and it mooed music as he cranked away. Another bovine's teeth became a xylophone on which he beat out a tune. In short, Willie had what its more pretentious competitors lacked—energy and freedom. And its creator was on his way to fame, riches and immortality.   —*By Richard Schickel*

CENSORED
Germany banned a Mickey flick in 1931 because "the wearing of German military helmets by an army of cats which oppose an army of mice is offensive to national dignity"

Nov. 18, 1928

WALT DISNEY'S MICKEY MOUSE in STEAMBOAT WILLIE

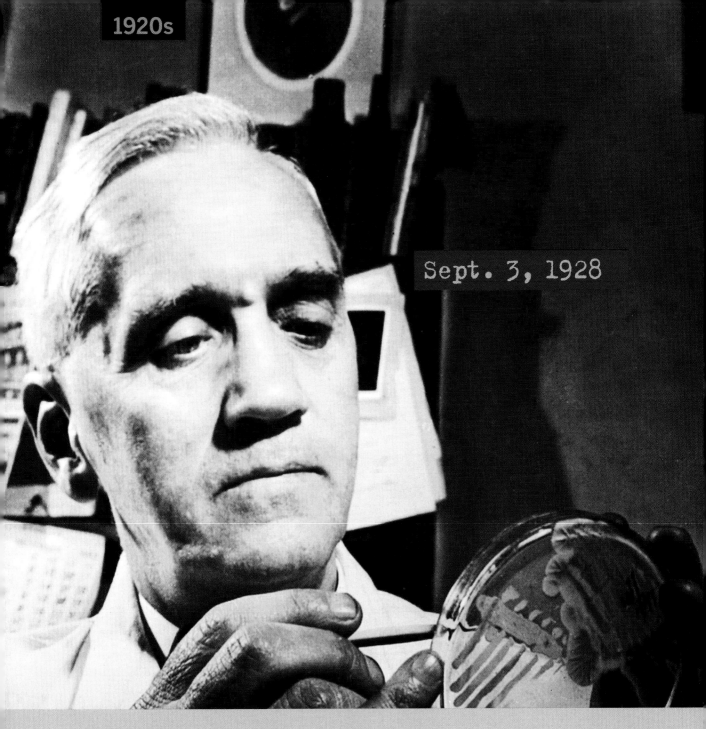

Sept. 3, 1928

In Matter's Decay, A Medical Miracle

For the first 2 million years or so of human history, bacterial infections—syphilis, festering wounds, scarlet fever, pneumonia—were often tantamount to a death sentence. But one London morning, humanity got a dramatic reprieve when a Scottish researcher named Alexander Fleming happened to glance at some Petri dishes about to be sterilized for reuse and said, "That's funny."

Fleming, who had seen the horrors of infection during World War I, was searching for a safe, powerful antibiotic. So far, he had found only a weak one, called lysozyme, extracted from body fluids. But when he looked at the dishes, Fleming noticed that the bacterial cultures were dying off. The killer: "mold juice," as he called it, the product of spores that had probably wafted in from a lab downstairs. Fleming determined that the spores were *Penicillium notatum* and renamed the juice penicillin. It would be a decade, however, before other scientists noticed Fleming's work, purified penicillin and turned it into a miracle drug.

—By Michael Lemonick

HERO BY ACCIDENT
Fleming examines a penicillin culture in a Petri dish in 1930

Wall Street's Bad, Bad Fall

Tales of suicides have been grossly overstated. But it was a day that shredded fortunes. The preceding week had already seen such huge waves of panic selling that Police Commissioner Grover Whalen stationed an extra 500 cops on the increasingly rowdy streets of New York City's Financial District. On Oct. 29, the panic that had possessed speculators and individuals was joined at the opening bell by traders for giant institutions. Blue chips like Standard Oil and Westinghouse gapped lower on massive trading volume. On a whim, a messenger bid for 100 shares of White Sewing Machine at $1—and in the absence of any other buyers, got it. The stock had been as high as $48 some months earlier.

The heads of New York's biggest banks had pledged $20 million each to support prices. But at a noonday meeting, they concluded that they could not stop the declines. In fact, one of the bankers, Albert Wiggin of Chase Bank, by means of a personal account had quietly sold the market short. The Dow would ultimately fall 89%—12% the day of the Crash—ushering in the Great Depression.

—*By Daniel Kadlec*

Oct. 29, 1929

BETTMANN CORBIS

BETTMANN CORBIS

READ ALL ABOUT IT
With "the tape" running hours late, an anxious crowd outside the New York Stock Exchange, above, learns details of the market's severe drop in the evening newspaper. Left, the wild ride of the '20s is officially over—and one of its symbols is already on sale

$100 WILL BUY THIS CAR MUST HAVE CASH LOST ALL ON THE STOCK MARKET

BETTMANN CORBIS (2)

CLARENCE DARROW AND WILLIAM JENNINGS BRYAN

On July 20, 1925, at the Scopes trial on teaching evolution in Tennessee schools, Darrow called prosecution counsel Bryan to the stand, as an expert on the Bible. Two hours later, after a barrage of questions that illustrated the folly of literal readings of the Bible, Bryan's reputation was in tatters

Fateful Meetings

OLIVER HARDY AND STAN LAUREL

In the 1921 silent short *A Lucky Dog*, star Laurel bends over to pet the titular pooch when his backside bumps into something large, round, and soft— the rump of masked bandit Hardy. But Hollywood's original odd couple didn't tie the knot until 1927's *Putting Pants on Philip*

PHOTOFEST

SUZANNE LENGLEN AND HELEN WILLS

The two greatest female tennis players of their day— the Ali and Frazier of the jazz age—squared off on the French Riviera on the afternoon of Feb. 16, 1926. France's flamboyant Lenglen, left, beat America's no-nonsense Wills in two sets, only to collapse in tears when the match was over

Snapshots

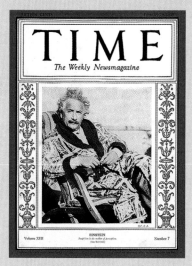

■ Albert Einstein

Dr. and Mrs. Einstein are cousins. March 14 he will be 50 years old. She is almost that age. A level-headed practical woman, she finds her philosophizing husband no nuisance. Said she: "Professor Einstein is not eccentric. He wears stiff collars without protest. He hardly ever mislays things. At least, not more than most men. He knows when it's time for lunch and dinner." **—Feb. 18, 1929**

■ Amy Lowell

Renowned as critic and poet, she begins her work at twelve at night, continues till eight in the morning, smokes cigars the while. She owns one of the most valuable collections of Keatsiana in the world. **—May 7, 1928**

■ Walter Chrysler

Early in August, Mr. Chrysler brought out another new car, called the De Soto. In autumn came the news that he was going to build the world's tallest skyscraper, a 68-story colossus towering more than 800 feet above Lexington Ave. and 42nd St., Manhattan. Almost incidentally, he brought out a new line of commercial cars— the Fargo "Packets" and "Clippers."

The doings of Walter P. Chrysler, already prodigious, now became fabulous. People said that this torpedo-headed dynamo from Detroit ... was building a facsimile and four-square competitor of mighty General Motors and that he was going to house it in a skyscraper where it could peer down at the General Motors Building on Broadway.   **—Jan. 7, 1929**

■ Calvin Coolidge

Spick and span in steel gray, bright brass and Sunday "whites," the *Texas*, her captain & crew, will be waiting for the President at Key West to ferry him to Havana. A squadron of destroyers is the guard of honor. When newsgatherers last week saw bigger & better portholes being built into the most sumptuous suite on the *Texas* at the Brooklyn Navy Yard, they inferred it was in honor of the President. But a deck officer said: "Not at all! We're putting those in for our Admiral!" Caesar is not greater to his sailors than his chief of steel-plated triremes.   **—Jan. 16, 1928**

■ Charlie Chaplin

His first efforts to be funny in celluloid were dismal. Keystone directors feared that he was overpaid, offered to cancel the contract. Chaplin told Rosco Arbuckle, the now deposed cinema clown, that he needed a pair of shoes. Arbuckle tossed him a pair of his own enormous brogues: "Perfect fit!" Chaplin put them on, cocked his battered derby over his ear, twisted the ends of his mustache. His face was very sad. He attempted a jaunty walk which became, inevitably, a heart-breaking waddle. He put his hand on the seat of his trousers, spun on his heel. Arbuckle told him that he was almost funny. Such was the research that led Chaplin to "create a figure that would be a living satire on every human vanity." **—July 6, 1925**

OCT. 1, 1932 After homering off Chicago Cubs pitcher Charlie Root in the first inning of a World Series game, Babe Ruth (above, in 1934) seemed to gesture to center field when he next faced Root—and sent the first pitch sailing into the Wrigley Field bleachers

APRIL 9, 1939
Banned because of her race from performing in a Washington concert hall owned by the Daughters of the American Revolution, contralto Marian Anderson sings to a crowd of 75,000 at the Lincoln Memorial

193

"Once I built a railroad, made it run" … the roaring shriek of the '20s seemed far away to Americans slogging through the Depression. Railroads, once fast lanes to the future, now offered shelter to hobos and tramps. Overseas, Europeans were sinking into a dark time of fascism and war

APRIL 30, 1939
With global war nearing and too many Americans on the dole, visitors to the World's Fair in New York City loved Futurama, the rosy vision of life in 1960 on view at the General Motors pavilion

0s

A Disobedient Holy Man Defies a Global Empire

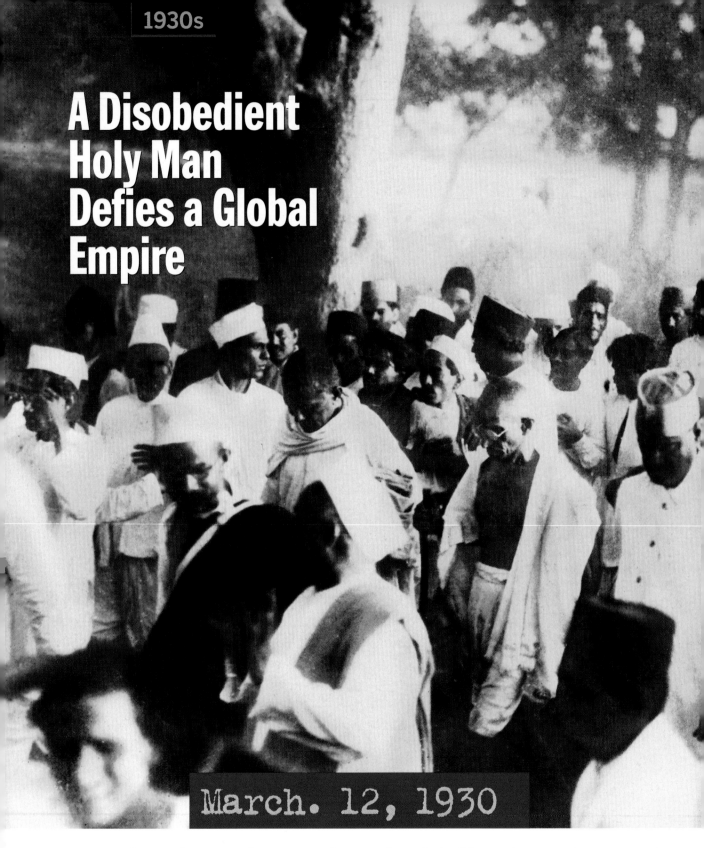

March. 12, 1930

Soon after saying his customary dawn prayers, Mahatma Gandhi emerged from his ashram to greet a crowd of thousands gathered to witness the start of his latest and most defiant protest against the "curse" of British rule. A volunteer band raised its horns and, it was reported, blared a few bars of *God Save the King* before it apparently dawned on the Indian musicians that a rousing salute to the English sovereign was not the most appropriate send-off for their first strides toward independence. Their fading notes were overtaken by the sound of coconuts being smashed together, a traditional Hindu sign of devotion.

Gandhi, leaning on a lacquered bamboo staff, soon set out along the winding, dusty road. His destination: Dandi, 240 miles away, where 25 days later he would collect a few grains

RESIST! Gandhi's strategies guided Mandela, King and Walesa to success

FOOT SOLDIERS Gandhi's 240-mile journey marked the start of colonialism's demise

■ Gandhi's Disciples

The tactics developed so successfully by Mohandas Gandhi in his struggle to win independence for India became the template for nonviolent social change around the world. The recipe: mass civil disobedience and passive resistance that sparked reprisals from the authorities, thus dramatizing injustice and providing the publicity needed to win over hearts and minds.

Three winners of the Nobel Peace Prize—Nelson Mandela, the Rev. Martin Luther King Jr. and Lech Walesa—cited Gandhi as a key influence in their own crusades. Only Mandela, who was a strong disciple of Gandhi's in his early years, departed from the path of nonviolence. In 1961 he helped found Umkhonto we Sizwe (Spear of the Nation), a faction of the African National Congress that advocated violent resistance against South Africa's government. But his days as a guerrilla were brief: after 17 months on the lam (when he was called the "Black Pimpernel"), he was arrested and jailed—for 27 years.

of salt in defiance of the British tax that forced locals to pay prices for the essential compound that were said to be up to 2,000% greater than its production costs. Following his lead, thousands of Indian villagers waded into the sea to extract salt themselves. Thus began Gandhi's campaign of nonviolent civil disobedience—and the beginning of the end of the British Empire. —*By Amanda Bower*

What TIME Said Then

Mr. Gandhi sank to the ground, [he] had to have cold compresses applied to his head, his legs swabbed with ointment, before he could proceed … Newsgatherers reported they did not believe the emaciated saint would be physically able to go much farther. —*March 24, 1930*

TEACHING
Morning Bible class at a federal workers' camp in New Jersey, 1942

BUILDING
Flood-control work on the Arkansas River, 1939

CREATING
Painting a mural in New York City, 1940

■ Workin' for the Man

At their birth, Franklin D. Roosevelt's New Deal programs were something entirely alien to the American scene. Products of a gigantic national experiment in social engineering, the new federal works projects had F.D.R.'s Republican adversaries sputtering about socialism, but the programs also inspired and enthralled many Americans, who had swept Roosevelt into office with a landslide mandate for change. Under an "alphabet soup" of New Deal agencies, tens of thousands of unemployed Americans now found themselves rolling up their sleeves to work for Uncle Sam.

The high tide of the New Deal may be long past, but if you seek its memorials, look around: its fruits are still evident in cities and towns across America, in highways and bridges, post offices and schools, dams and swimming pools. The state guidebooks created by the WPA Writers Program— written anonymously by some of the era's most gifted journalists—remain lively, loving tributes to America's regional diversity.

HOPELESS
A young mother at a migrant camp in California

What TIME Said Then

They sat on benches. They filled bare trees. They perched on roof tops. But for all the flags and music and ceremony, they were not a happy, carefree crowd. Their bank accounts were frozen by a national moratorium.
— *March 13, 1933*

Launching the New Deal

March 4, 1933

The day was cold and somber. Nearly a quarter of the United States labor force was out of work. Banks had shut their doors. Farms were going belly up. Breadlines snaked through city streets. Standing jut jawed at the lectern before the Capitol's assembled throng on his first Inauguration Day, Franklin Delano Roosevelt countered the sense of helplessness, telling the shaken nation, "The only thing we have to fear is fear itself." He then outlined a plan of economic revolution: bank and stock-market reforms, public-works programs, and emergency relief for the nation's farmers.

But the day's solemnity made room for celebration too, as Roosevelt answered cheers by shaking his hands over his head like a prizefighter. Later he wagged his top hat at marchers in the Inauguration parade, including four men pushing lawn mowers, a gibe at outgoing President Hoover's remark that if Democrats won, grass would grow in the streets.

— *By Margot Roosevelt*

CINEMA CZAR:
Hays, a former
Postmaster
General, put the
strict film code
into effect

July 1, 1934

CINEMAMA
Mae West
had to tone
down her
sassy style to
suit the new
strictures

Movies' Moral Crackdown

Goodness, what beautiful diamonds!" a hatcheck girl says to Mae West, who purrs, "Goodness had nothin' to do with it, dearie." That line, from West's 1932 *Night After Night*, embodied the saucy spirit of early talkies. Now that Hollywood could speak, it did so in the tart cadences of fast-talking men and faster women. This freedom created fresh stars (James Cagney, Barbara Stanwyck, Jean Harlow) and a sexual impudence that riled the burghers of propriety. In 1934 the potent Roman Catholic lobby formed the Legion of Decency to rate films. Soon after, Will Hays, the industry's political and moral arbiter, called on Joseph Breen, a prominent Catholic, to enforce a rigorous production code. Studios rushed to sanitize some projects (West got married at the end of *Belle of the Nineties*) and dump others (MGM had to wait 12 years to film *The Postman Always Rings Twice*). Moviegoers that summer Sunday may have been shocked by the sudden absence of shocking dialogue and situations. But filmmakers evolved a new "code," one that traded starkness for subtlety. Audiences quickly learned this covert language in which a woman's coy smile was its own double entendre, and a kiss was never just a kiss.

—By Richard Corliss

What TIME Said Then

A Presbyterian elder whose solid connections helped get him his job, Tsar Hays has long mollified church people and women's clubs with bland promises of reform. *— July 2, 1934*

AA Takes Its First Steps

Bill Wilson, a stockbroker and a drunk from Brooklyn, N.Y., thought he had found the secret of kicking the bottle. But on a business trip to Akron, Ohio, he found himself outside a bar, tempted and desperate. In the past, he had fought the urge by talking to other alcoholics, who truly understood his struggle. Through a church group, he found local surgeon Robert Holbrook Smith.

Dr. Bob and Bill W., as Alcoholics Anonymous members know them, promised to keep each other sober, following Bill W.'s strategy: a simple set of principles—later refined into 12 steps—that would become the foundation of America's self-help culture. Alcoholics, he said, must admit they are powerless over their addiction. They must make amends to all those they have harmed. And they must submit to God—however they define the deity.

The advice did not immediately take. Dr. Bob went to Atlantic City, N.J., for a convention; several days later, he showed up at the Akron train station, smashed. On June 10, the dried-out but still jittery doctor was due in surgery. That morning, Bill W. gave Dr. Bob a bottle of beer—to steady his scalpel hand. The operation was a success. The beer was Dr. Bob's last. And the two men pledged that day to work to bring Bill W.'s principles to other alcoholics, one day at a time.
—**By James Poniewozik**

DRIED-OUT DUO
Bill W., right, in his kitchen, 1952; at Dr. Bob's home, late 1930s, with Bill W. on the right

June 10, 1935

AA WORLD SERVICES, INC.; DR. BOB'S HOME/AKRON, OHIO

Racing Against Racism, Owens Outruns Hitler

I was the captain of the U.S. marathon team in the 1936 Olympics and a special friend of Jesse Owens'. On the boat going to Germany, Jesse said to me, "I want to go up to the deck and exercise, but I don't have any shoes." So I said, "I don't think my shoes will fit you." But that didn't stop him. He tried to get a shoe on, but his foot was so large, it broke my shoe right in half. He apologized, and I got it sewed up. It cost me 50¢, and I got a souvenir.

When I finished the marathon, Hitler waved to me, and I thumbed my nose at him. That's my claim to fame. But Jesse told me, "Kelley, Hitler waved to me, and I waved back." That's actually what happencd. When he won his fourth medal that day, after setting three world records, Jesse was the hero of the whole Games. To everyone. Except for Hitler. The dictator looked almost unbeatable at the time, but Jesse's victories upset his theory about an Aryan master race.

Jesse Owens was the greatest track athlete we have ever had. But he was also a great hero for everybody concerned. I'm proud to have been his friend. **—By John Kelley**

Kelley, 95, competed in 61 Boston Marathons and won two.

Birth of the Superhero

Comic books were just a few years old when the red-caped figure, lifting a 2-ton car as if it were lawn furniture, graced the cover of *Action Comics No. 1.* Superman was the creation of Cleveland teenagers Jerry Siegel (writer) and Joe Shuster (illustrator). They envisioned him in 1932 and for six fruitless years tried to get him into print.

In early 1938, comics publisher Max Gaines (whose son Bill would publish *Mad* in the '50s) recommended the lads to DC Comics. Finally someone said yes. From that first issue, the character was fully formed: he could "hurdle a 20-story building … run faster than an express train …" and still, as Clark Kent, could never manage to impress newsgal Lois Lane.

The final panel seemed boastful: "Superman is destined to reshape the destiny of a world!" But it was simply prophetic. To Americans deep in an economic Depression and listening to the drumbeats of European war, the Man of Steel offered both escape and hope. Readers loved him, and, in a trice, gaudy imitations (Batman, Wonder Woman, Captain America) were clogging the racks. Superman spun off into half a dozen TV series and several generations of movies; his example inspired the Daredevils and Spider-Men of a later era. Yet Siegel and Shuster saw little of the profit DC made from their character. Not until 1975 did the company agree to pay a modest annuity to the men who had created the comics' first and most enduring superhero.

—By Richard Corliss

MASTERLY: Owens dusts the pack in the 100-m dash at the '36 Olympics

BLACK STAR

April 15, 1938

ACTION COMICS

10¢

SUPERMAN AND ALL RELATED CHARACTERS AND ELEMENTS ARE TRADEMARKS AND © DC COMICS

What TIME Said Then

At the Owens cabana in the Olympic Village, awed rivals crowded to feel the Owens muscles, get the Owens autograph … over the radio [his mother] described her son: "Jesse was always a face boy … When a problem came up, he always faced it." —*Aug. 17, 1936*

RUINS: A Jewish shop in Berlin rampaged by Nazis during the attacks of Kristallnacht

Nov. 9, 1938

The Night When Hope Shattered

In 1938 I was 21, living in Würzburg in southern Germany and studying at the Jewish Teachers' Seminary. I was supposed to have an exam on Nov. 10, the final one before I would have got my diploma that would have made me a Hebrew teacher. So on the ninth, I headed home early in the evening and went to bed at 9 so I would be refreshed the next morning. We had already heard a few days before about the assassination of Ernst vom Rath, an official at the German embassy in Paris, killed by a Polish Jew, and it was a very bad omen.

Everything went fine until about 2:30 in the morning, when we were awakened by a big crash. I got up and didn't know what might have happened. I lived in a large dormitory room with two friends. I thought that it was something terrible and that we should be ready to meet the emergency. We packed our valises in case we needed to leave. We heard people coming closer, and we tried to lock our door. I don't know if we opened it or if they broke it, but they were Nazis dressed as civilians. They said, "Throw your bags against the windows." And they went down the hall and threw three typewriters against the windows, and then they came back and went to the big dormitory room and broke more things, like the faucets in the sink and the hanging lamps.

About 6 the next morning, a whole group of people came, as if they were looking at a museum, to enjoy themselves and see what the Nazis had done in our building. One man, another Nazi in civilian clothes, told us to go outside and form a line five abreast in the cobblestone street. As we walked along, the civilians at the side spat at us and called us names. We passed by the burning synagogue as they led us to the prison, and all these onlookers, they were laughing, they were shouting, and they were spitting.

Kristallnacht was a turning point because up to that time, the Nazis did not openly incite the whole population to kill publicly. Before, people were killed secretly and individually, but this happened openly. After that night, the whole world knew it would not get better at all, and Jews knew only a dark future. It was called the "Night of Broken Glass," but it was more than that. You can clean up glass, but you cannot do that with people. **—By Jacob G. Wiener**

Rabbi Wiener, 86, gives tours at the U.S. Holocaust Memorial Museum.

Unearthing the King's Fortune

NESTOR SANDER COLLECTION—SAUDI ARAMCO/PADIA

The King of Saudi Arabia, Abd-al-Aziz ibn Saud, had authorized a team of American engineers to explore the trackless desert bordering the Persian Gulf, an arid landscape marked only by the occasional palm-fringed oasis. He hoped they would find water. A tribal leader with precarious finances, Ibn Saud believed the Americans might discover places where he could refresh his warriors' horses and camels. But the team, from Standard Oil of California, had something else on its mind. Oil had been discovered in other countries in the region, and the engineers thought they would find more in Saudi Arabia. Over several years, they drilled more than half a dozen holes without result. In desperation, they decided to dig deeper at well No. 7. They plumbed to a depth of 4,727 ft. and finally hit what would turn out to be the largest supply of crude oil in the world.

The King did not appear to appreciate the news fully at first. It was an entire year after the discovery when he and his retinue arrived in a caravan of 400 automobiles at the pumping station of Ras Tanura to witness the first tanker hauling away its cargo of Saudi crude. Henceforth the King would no longer rely for income on the pilgrims arriving in Mecca, Islam's holiest city. And his kingdom's petroleum wealth would soon emerge as a crucial factor in Middle East politics and the bargaining over global energy supplies.   —**By Adam Zagorin**

PAY DIRT **Above, crude gushes from Damman No. 7, the first of the Saudi wells to produce oil. Below, U.S. engineers lay pipe to move the oil to Saudi ports**

March 3, 1938

Hitler Storms Into Poland

Sept. 1, 1939

BRUTE FORCE With stunning rapidity, German troops marched through the streets of Polish towns and adorned buildings with swastikas

Adolf Hitler, by some reports, spent the week before the invasion of Poland confined to the Reich Chancellery, the opulent quarter-mile edifice he had built to symbolize Germany's might. During that time, he subsisted on a spartan diet of vegetables, buttered bread and his custom-brewed 1%-alcohol beer. He slept little, usually going to bed at sunrise.

The border fighting began under cover of night. By dawn the Polish city of Dirschau was under siege, and it was official: Germany had attacked its neighbor. At 10 a.m. Hitler finally emerged from his fortress. He was wearing a new suit specially tailored for the occasion; it was lighter gray than the regular army uniform, with shiny gold buttons, a swastika and the Iron Cross medal he had won in the previous World War.

As more than 1 million troops flooded into Poland and began taking civilian prisoners, Hitler drove to the Reichstag to

MOVE IT! Germany's few motorized divisions hurled war into a new, faster era

GUDERIAN: Prophet of accelerated war

F A Polish girl mourns lder sister, killed by ng German aircraft

■ Shock and Awe, 1939

When Adolf Hitler's war machine smashed its way into Poland, the world learned a new word: *blitzkrieg*. The Wehrmacht's "lightning war" hurtled combat into fast-forward, with swooping attacks by dive-bombing fighter planes and rapid penetration by mechanized tanks and artillery. Credit for the breakthrough was given to General Heinz Guderian, the panzer leader who was Germany's foremost advocate of mechanized warfare.

That's the standard story. But in recent years, some historians have described the blitzkrieg as a triumph more of Nazi propaganda than of German arms. Only eight of the 54 divisions that attacked Poland were truly mechanized—the 46 others were old-fashioned infantry divisions that moved no faster than the mules that hauled their howitzers and bratwurst. Their day's supply needs: 20 tons of petroleum and 50 tons of oats and hay. But by placing their few motorized divisions in the vanguard—and ceaselessly publicizing their frightening new strategy—the Germans created a myth of invincibility that would serve them well over the next few years.

appear before the Parliament. "I myself am today, and will be from now on, nothing but the soldier of the German Reich," he said. "I shall not take off this uniform until we have achieved victory." Within two days Britain and France jumped to Poland's defense, and World War II was under way in Europe. Five and a half years—and millions of deaths—later, Hitler died in his underground bunker in Berlin, with his uniform on. 　　　　　　　　　　**—By Jodie Morse**

What TIME Said Then

Several German planes had bombed a farmhouse. They went away, and seven Polish women who were desperately in need of food went out to scratch for potatoes. But the planes ... doubled back and, flying as low as 200 feet, opened up their machine guns. — *Oct. 16, 1939*

HULTON ARCHIVE—GETTY

BONNIE PARKER AND CLYDE BARROW On June 5, 1930, Barrow, 20, visited a girlfriend in Dallas and went into the kitchen for some cocoa. There he met Parker, 19, and fell hard. The duo's faux populist crime sprees inspired a better film than they deserved

Fateful Meetings

JOSEPH STALIN AND JOACHIM VON RIBBENTROP The Kremlin boss was ready to deal on Aug. 23, 1939, when he met in secret with Germany's Foreign Minister. After a few hours, champagne glasses clinked as Stalin toasted Adolf Hitler; the nonaggression pact was sealed. Within a week, Germany would attack Poland and plunge Europe into a six-year war

BETTMANN CORBIS

FRED ASTAIRE AND GINGER ROGERS First time out, it was Ginger and Fred: she was billed fourth, he fifth in *Flying Down to Rio*. They were filler, but when they stepped out in the musical number *The Carioca*, *it was clear* that they were an ideal match. Eight timeless films followed

Snapshots

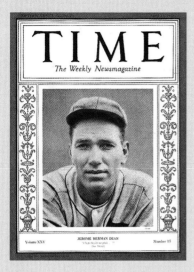

■ Dizzy Dean

When he first joined the Cardinals, pitcher Dean squandered his money so foolishly that he was put on an allowance of $1 a day. He registered at three hotels, slept in whichever one was closest when he felt tired. On a blistering day in St. Louis last year, he lit a bonfire in front of his team's dugout, wrapped himself in a blanket, pretended to be an Indian.
—April 15, 1935

■ Fiorello LaGuardia

He took a down-at-heel city and gave it desperately needed equipment, scores of new school buildings, sewage plants, incinerators, more than double the number of playgrounds and dental clinics for children. **—Aug. 2, 1937**

■ Huey Long

"There may be smarter men than me but they ain't in Louisiana," Huey Long likes to brag. His enemies will agree that he is no fool but they will also contend that his smartness is far from admirable. He has developed a political technique in which he is too intelligent to believe himself. Impervious to insult, he knows the trick of playing politics in its rawest, crudest form and he plays it with a vim, dash and audacity that stagger men with public sensibilities. The night the Legislature passed his cotton bill, he sent out for a cotton nightshirt. Near midnight he had himself photographed in it signing the bill. "Now I can take this damn thing off!" he exploded afterwards as he climbed back into his silk pajamas. **—Oct. 3, 1932**

■ Shirley Temple

It might seem natural for the most celebrated child alive to be in private life the most objectionable sample of precocity, weight for age, who ever gave sharp answers to her betters. Such is not the case. Disappointing as the case may be to persons judicious enough to distrust the customary vaporings of cinema fan magazines, Shirley Temple is actually a peewee paragon who not only obeys her mother, likes her work, rarely cries and is never sick, but even likes raw carrots, eats spinach with enthusiam and expresses active relish for the taste of castor oil. **—April 27, 1936**

■ Frank Lloyd Wright

Facing southwest over the Wisconsin River valley a big, long house folds around the summit of one hill, its roof lines parallel to the line of ridges, its masonry the same red-yellow sandstone that crops out in ledges along the stream. Its name is Taliesin, a Welsh word meaning "shining brow." For the past five years Taliesen has been a workshop, farm and studio for more than a score of apprentices who are interested in architecture as Frank Lloyd Wright understands it. During its first winter the Taliesin Fellowship spent much of its time cutting wood in two shifts to keep the fires going. Since then, its life has been less defensive. After nearly a decade, the master of Taliesin has again had work in hand. **—Jan. 17, 1938**

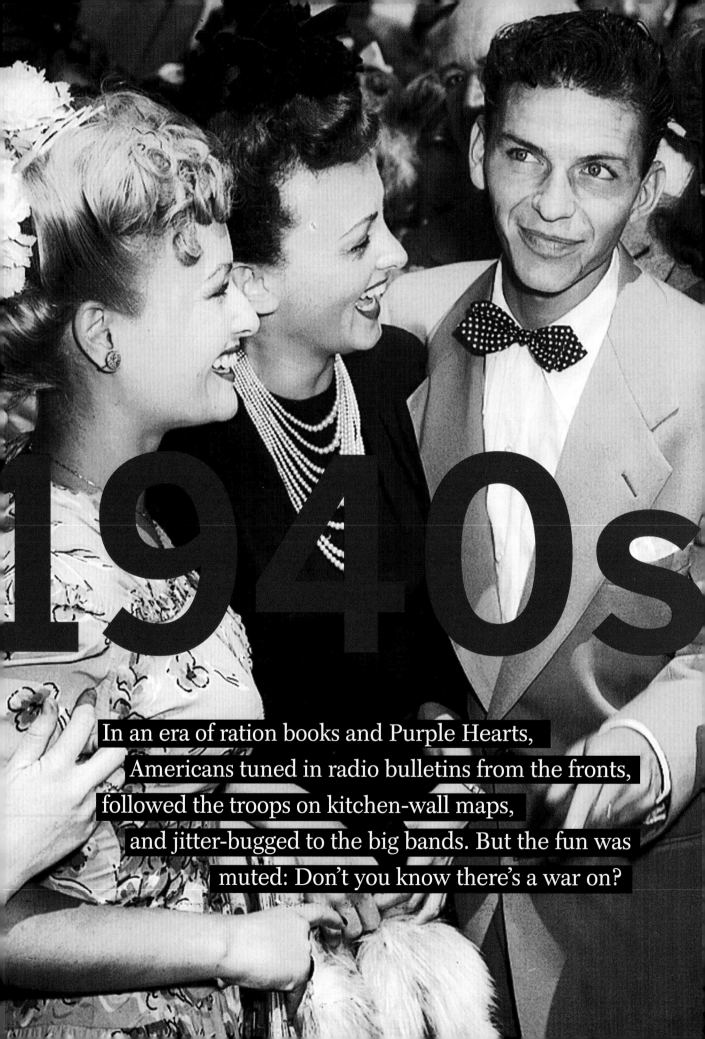

1940s

In an era of ration books and Purple Hearts, Americans tuned in radio bulletins from the fronts, followed the troops on kitchen-wall maps, and jitter-bugged to the big bands. But the fun was muted: Don't you know there's a war on?

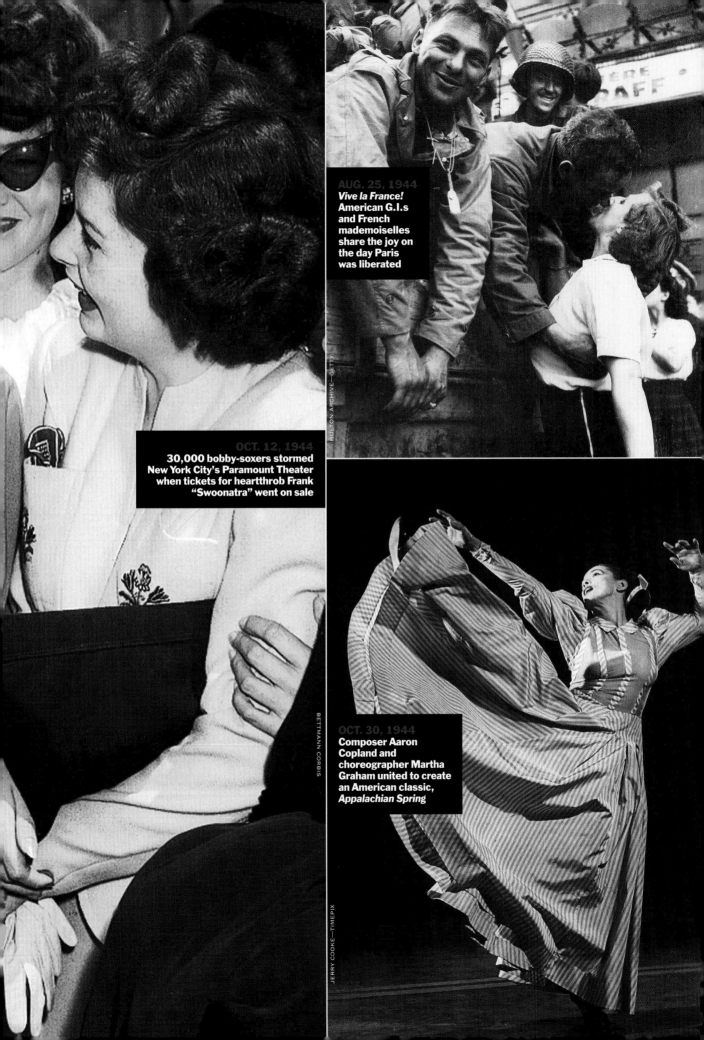

AUG. 25, 1944
Vive la France!
American G.I.s
and French
mademoiselles
share the joy on
the day Paris
was liberated

OCT. 12, 1944
30,000 bobby-soxers stormed
New York City's Paramount Theater
when tickets for heartthrob Frank
"Swoonatra" went on sale

OCT. 30, 1944
Composer Aaron
Copland and
choreographer Martha
Graham united to create
an American classic,
Appalachian Spring

May 10, 1940

Fighting Words

Naming Winston Churchill as Man of the Year 1940 some six months after he took power in Britain's darkest hour, TIME observed of the British leader:

"Adolf Hitler and Winston Churchill are the two men alive in the world today who best understand the power of words as weapons of warfare. Their techniques are different. Hitler uses words as poison gas; Churchill uses them as a broadsword. On May 13, 1940, in his first statement as Prime Minister to the British House of Commons, Winston Leonard Spencer Churchill declared: 'I have nothing to offer but blood, toil, tears and sweat.' Those eleven burning words summed up the nature of Britain's war, turned Britain's back on the weaknesses of the past, set her face toward the unknown future. Because of them the rest of that speech has been forgotten. It should not be forgotten … After a brief report on his Government, Churchill said: 'You ask, what is our policy? I say it is to wage war by land, sea and air—war with all our might and with all the strength God has given us—and to wage war against a monstrous tyranny never surpassed in the dark, lamentable catalogue of human crime. That is our policy.' "

Said TIME: "Churchill gave his countrymen exactly what he promised them— blood, toil, tears, sweat—and one thing more: untold courage."

HULTON ARCHIVE/GETTY IMAGES

THE GREAT ESCAPE: Only weeks after Churchill took office, some 220,000 British and 110,000 French troops were safely evacuated from Dunkirk in Belgium, allowing the allies to fight on

What TIME Said Then

Although Prime Minister Churchill included his predecessor in his war Cabinet, the public career of Neville Chamberrlain was all but ended when he surrendered his seals of office, the most specactacular failure in English political history since Palmerston. —*May 20, 1940*

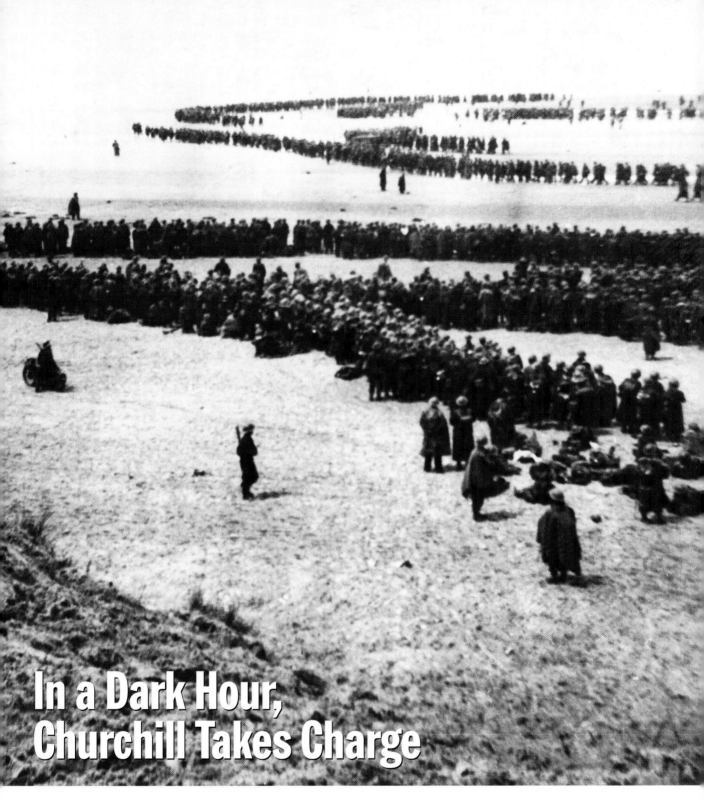

In a Dark Hour, Churchill Takes Charge

R arely have a man and a moment been so wonderfully matched as in May 1940, when Winston Churchill became Prime Minister of Britain. His ascension was improbable. Churchill spent the 1930s in the political wilderness, calling for rearmament against Germany and, on his return to government in 1939, was limited to control of the navy. But military disasters such as the Nazi seizure of Norwegian ports convinced the British public that Neville Chamberlain was not up to the job of fighting a war. By the night of May 8, after a stormy debate in the House of Commons, Chamberlain's position had become untenable. The opposition Labour Party declared it would serve in a government of national unity only if it were led by Churchill, and on the evening of May 10, as German troops massed against France, he accepted office from King George VI. Three days later, Churchill promised Britain only "blood, toil, tears and sweat." What he gave his country, above all, was leadership. **—By Michael Elliott**

What I Saw At Pearl Harbor

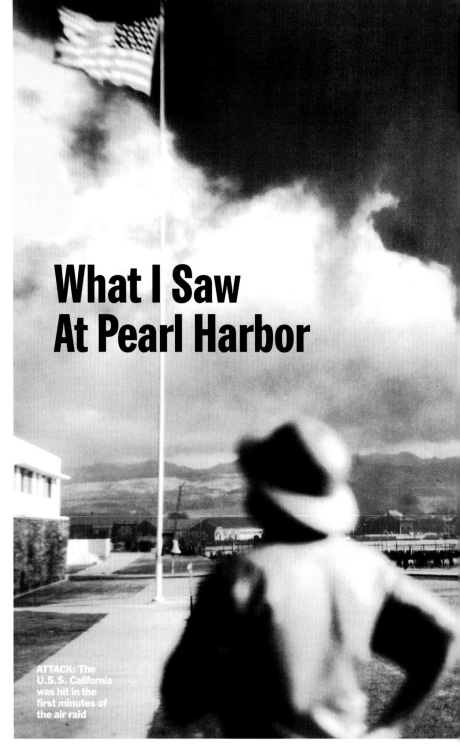

ATTACK: The U.S.S. *California* was hit in the first minutes of the air raid

Aas the Zeroes flew overhead on that lazy Sunday morning, some of my neighbors in the hills on Oahu waved at the planes, not realizing that they were the enemy and that this would be the day that would go down in infamy. My family and I were having breakfast that morning, and as the eldest son in a family of Japanese immigrants, I was given a special treat: hotcakes. But the noise was inescapable. The BANG BANG BANG became a resounding BOOM BOOM BOOM. I tried to assuage the family's fears, saying it must be only one of the weekly U.S. military exercises. Suddenly, an earth shaking VAROOOM! rattled our flimsy home. I immediately jumped from my chair and started running through the rice fields and over the railroad tracks until I was standing on the shore with the water lapping at my slippers. Across lay Pearl Harbor.

I watched as one of the battleships, perhaps the *Arizona*, went up in flames, soon blackened by huge funnels of clouds shooting skyward. The *West Virginia* and the *California* started to explode in a chain reaction. I soon heard the RAT-TAT-TAT of machine guns and squads of planes starting to dive-bomb the destroyers and cruisers nearest shore. I saw a large plane fly low over the water from the direction of Honolulu into battleship row and drop a torpedo toward the middle of the ships. The plane then turned toward Aiea, my hometown, hugging the surface of the water to avoid antiaircraft fire. As the plane flew a few hundred feet over my head, I saw the pilot with a canvas helmet and large goggles over his eyes looking down at me. As the plane headed north toward the mountains, I saw Japan's insignia, the Rising Sun. "How dare they come over and attack our land and country?" I raged to myself. Then a truckload of Marines came over and yelled at me to go home. On the way I saw a couple of Zeros on fire, plunging into the hills over my town.

The next day some of us sneaked over toward Pearl Harbor to see the damage. The long concrete pier along the shore was piled with stacks of bodies. The dead were later interred in a temporary cemetery nearby. National Guard soldiers soon took over and ordered every home to be blacked out at night. They shot at any light showing through the cracks. In our darkened, humid rooms, we huddled in dismay at the way our ancestral Japan had put a curse on all Japanese living in Hawaii. Other ethnic groups looked upon us as the enemy, not to be trusted. Our village elders soon got together to burn or destroy anything to do with Japan: photos of the Emperor, flags, swords and even shortwave radios that could be turned into transmitters. Still, the police on the sugar plantation where we lived led the FBI into Japanese homes. Many people were rounded up: language teachers and martial-arts instructors as well as labor leaders and businessmen. My future father-in-law was arrested at rifle point and incarcerated in one of 10 relocation camps. Second-generation Japanese-American soldiers in the 298th and

Dec. 7, 1941

YAMAMOTO: A
prescient prediction

AP/WIDE WORLD

CULVER PICTURES

■ The Giant Awakens

At 7 a.m. on April 18, 1943, a group of 16 U.S. long-range P-38 Lightning fighter planes went "wheels up" from Guadalcanal. Their mission: fly 400 miles across the Pacific to Bougainville in the Japanese-held Solomon Islands and shoot down a Japanese bomber carrying Admiral Isoroku Yamamoto.

Ironically, the brilliant naval strategist who planned Japan's stunning attack on Pearl Harbor had been hesitant about the wisdom of his nation's policy. "I fear all we have done is to awaken a sleeping giant," he confided to colleagues after the attack.

By the spring of 1943, the Americans were not only fully roused—they had broken Japan's naval code. When a message outlining Yamamoto's itinerary for his trip to the Solomons was intercepted, the Lightnings took to the air, flying just above the waves to avoid radar. After 2^1/$_2$ hours, the American pilots spotted two Japanese Mitsubishi (or "Betty") bombers and six Zero fighters. While 12 U.S. P-38s kept the escort of Zeros busy, the four others downed both Japanese bombers. Yamamoto was dead: in one stroke, the U.S. had not only punished Pearl Harbor's architect but also swept Japan's single best naval strategist from the battlefield.

A footnote: since the U.S. code breakthrough had to remain secret, the great deed remained under wraps. Until war's end, the official U.S. story was not that Yamamoto had been shot down, but that he had died in a crash.

299th Regiments were asked to leave the service, and their rifles were taken away.

Eventually, Japanese-American ROTC students formed the Victory Varsity Volunteers and joined the newly formed 442nd Regimental Combat Team. I would join too. I remember my parents saying "Don't bring shame to the family," adding that they would rather never see me again than have me avoid the dangers of serving in the Army. Using the old code of Bushido, the way of the samurai, they exhorted me to fight to the death for America. **—By Ronald Oba**

Oba, author of Men of Company F, 442nd Regimental Combat Team, *served in Italy and France.*

What TIME Said Then

Instantly, on news from Pearl Harbor, President Roosevelt ordered the Army and Navy, "Fight back!" The U.S., after 22 years and 25 days of peace, was at war ... [He] called a Cabinet meeting for 8:30 p.m. ... He had already finished the first draft of his war message ... There was no smile. The lines in his face were deeper. —*Dec. 15, 1941*

■ Talking Pictures

There are very few photographs of the early hours of the D-day invasion. The most familiar is probably Robert Capa's blurry picture of a U.S. soldier scrabbling his way ashore early in the fighting, below.

Forty-nine years after he died by stepping on a land mine while photographing the French war in Indochina, Capa, above, remains the paradigm of the combat photo-journalist. His account of landing with U.S. troops on D-day recalls the unadorned style of his good friend Ernest Hemingway: "I was going to Normandy on this nice, clean transport ship with a unit of the First Division. The food was good and we played poker. Once I filled an inside straight but I had four nines against me. Then just before six o'clock we were lowered in our LCVP and we started for the beach. It was rough and some of the boys were politely puking into paper bags. I always said this was a civilized invasion. We heard something popping around our boat but nobody paid any attention. We got out of the boat and started wading and then I saw men falling and had to push past their bodies. I said to myself, 'This is not so good.'"

PIX INC—TIMEPIX

HULTON ARCHIVE/GETTY IMAGES

ROBERT CAPA—MAGNUM PHOTOS

ALL ASHORE 1,465 U.S. soldiers died on D-day—fewer American lives than were lost at Pearl Harbor or in the 2001 strike on the World Trade Center

The landing craft disgorged, riflemen deployed. Beachmasters established their stations, directing the mounting traffic ... The Crusade was on ... At day's end the boats which had landed the greatest amphibious force in history began ferrying the wounded and the dead back to England. —*June 12, 1944*

I was 24 years old, the acting platoon leader for the 2nd Ranger Battalion, D Company. We were charged with one of the most dangerous missions that day, and we had been training for it since April. After we landed on the beach of Pointe du Hoc, which was between Omaha and Utah beaches, we were supposed to climb the 100-foot-high cliffs and take out the German cannons we believed were stationed there. The guns had a 10- to 12-mile range and were a danger to the forces landing at Utah and Omaha.

There were 22 people in my particular LCA [landing craft, artillery]. We were under fire as we neared the beach. When the ramp of the LCA went down, I was the first one to step out. As I was getting off, I was shot in my side, but the bullet only

June 6, 1944

D-Day: Saving a Continent

went through muscle—it didn't hit any joints—so I was able to keep going. When you're a leader, you've got to see to it that everything gets done. As long as you can stand up, you keep going. After getting shot, I stepped off the ramp and thought the water would be ankle deep, but I stepped into a shell crater, so I went down holding all my gear and was completely underwater. The other guys pulled me up, and we started our assault of the cliffs. We fired hooks, with ropes attached, onto the cliffs, and we set about climbing the ropes.

The Germans were firing down on us, sending mortars, and they were cutting the ropes. When we reached the top of the cliffs, we had to fight through the Germans and locate the huge guns. But they weren't there. They had been moved. We had to keep searching for them. The Germans were hiding in underground tunnels. Every time you turned around, one would pop up. I found the guns about a mile away in an apple orchard and rendered them inoperable by damaging them with grenades.

I wasn't really scared. I was the platoon leader and I had no time to think of myself. We had a very difficult mission, and we did a very fine job. All told, 150,000 Allied soldiers came ashore that day. But it had its cost. I landed with 225 other Rangers, and only 90 were left standing at the end of the battle.

—By Leonard Lomell

Lomell, a retired lawyer, lives in Toms River, N.J.

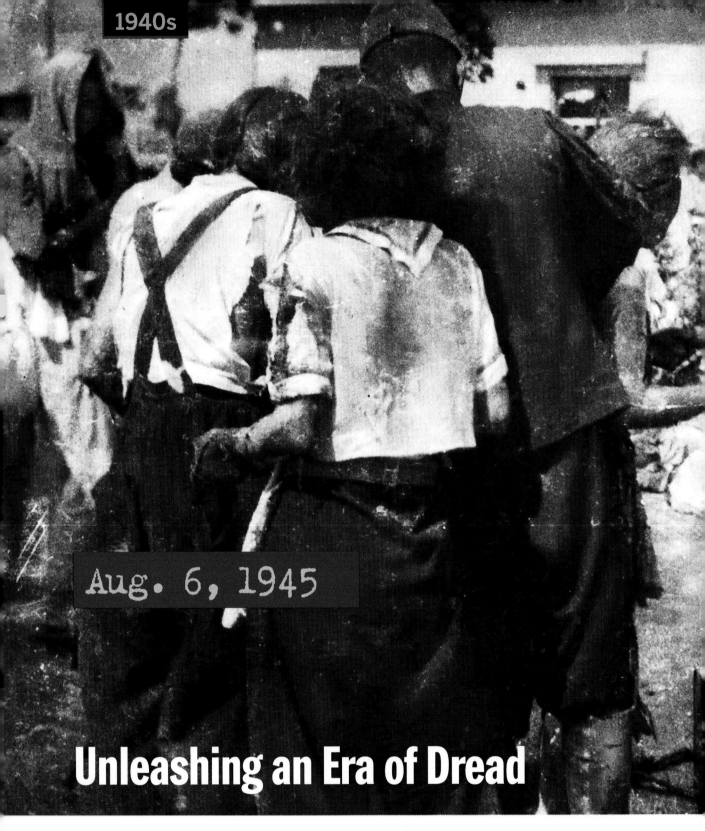

Aug. 6, 1945

Unleashing an Era of Dread

Emiko Okada was playing in the yard with her two little brothers when she saw the blinding light. Then came a boom and a blast that knocked her unconscious. When she came to, she recalled, "I felt like the sun was falling toward me." Her brothers wailed beside her, their bodies swollen with burns. Neighbors stumbled by, naked, skin hanging off them in shreds. Corpses littered the road. It was Aug. 6, 1945, in Hiroshima. No one in the south-

ern Japanese city had paid much attention to the distant buzz of three American B-29 bombers overhead. But one of them was the *Enola Gay*, and at 8:15 a.m. it dropped a single bomb that unleashed the "rain of ruin" President Truman had promised if Japan did not surrender.

An estimated one-third of the city's 350,000 residents were killed instantly. Many thousands more would die from the bomb's radioactive poison in the coming years. The

ORDEAL: A rare picture of survivors, taken just after the bomb was dropped

ALFRED EISENSTAEDT—TIMEPIX

■ The Outcast

When the Manhattan Project was America's most closely guarded secret, its director, Robert J. Oppenheimer, was indispensable. But once the atom bomb ended the war, America entered an era of fear. By the early 1950s, Oppenheimer— a Jewish, Ivy League liberal from New York City—had become a favorite target of U.S. red stalkers. Oppenheimer's ambivalence about building the hydrogen bomb sealed his fate. After a September 1953 hearing, the Atomic Energy Commission stripped him of his security clearance. The most damning testimony had come from a colleague: Edward Teller, the Hungarian-born physicist who envied the reverence "Oppie" inspired in fellow scientists. Teller went on to produce the hydrogen bomb. Oppenheimer never worked for the government again.

HULTON ARCHIVE—GETTY IMAGES

bomb turned glass to liquid, buildings to dust, and people to mere shadows etched on the ruins. A black rain fell. It looked like oil to Seiko Komatsu, then 9. He saw the rain soak his wounded grandparents. He had been having breakfast in their house when the bomb fell and gutted it. Three days later, the city of Nagasaki was destroyed by another atom bomb. Japan announced its unconditional surrender on Aug. 14.   **—By Lisa Takeuchi Cullen**

What TIME Said Then

The greatest and most terrible of wars ended in the echoes of an enormous event— an event so much more enormous that, relative to it, the war itself shrank to minor significance. The knowledge of victory was charged with sorrow and doubt as with joy and gratitude. —*Aug. 20, 1945*

April 15, 1947

Baseball Breaks The Color Line

The game wasn't a sellout. It lured 25,623 fans, more than half of them black, to the 32,000 seats of Brooklyn's Ebbets Field. What those present saw was a piece of history in nine innings: a black man playing in a major league game for the first time.

Of course, Jackie Robinson didn't break the color line in baseball all by himself. He needed Branch Rickey to do it. The president and general manager of the Brooklyn Dodgers was the one with the will and the power to upend the idiotic myopia of the sport's other sachems. (Were they afraid that blacks couldn't play baseball or afraid that they could play it too well?) Rickey had been searching for an athlete whose poise matched his skills, who could swallow the racist insults sure to be directed at him by players and fans—someone, Rickey told Robinson at their first meeting, "with guts enough not to fight back."

Robinson was the man. The first four-sport star at UCLA, an Army veteran, a budding Negro League phenom, Robinson neither smoke nor drank and possessed a heroic reserve off the field to complement his fiery resolve on it. As he stepped to the plate in a Dodgers' uniform, he was a mature 28 years old that April day. (By contrast, Derek Jeter was playing in his eighth major league season when he reached that age last June.) But in a magnificent 10-year Hall of Fame career Robinson made up for lost time—his and that of the great Negro League ballplayers who never got the chance to shine in the Bigs. When Robinson stepped onto the field, it was the day baseball finally earned the right to be called the national pastime.

—*By Richard Corliss*

When Freedom Bred Calamity

At the stroke of midnight hour, when the world sleeps, India will awake to life and freedom." So declared Jawaharlal Nehru in his speech on the eve of his nation's independence from Britain. In New Delhi the next day, the celebrating crowd was so huge that Nehru, the new Prime Minister, had to fight his way to the grandstand. He was worried for the safety of his friends, the last British viceroy Lord Mountbatten, a cousin of England's monarch, and his wife Edwina, with whom Nehru was secretly enamored. But Mountbatten himself knew of another secret that would cause great grief.

Muslims and Hindus were inheriting a divided subcontinent from Britain, made up of Pakistan and India. Already the legalistic partition had led to deadly rioting. But one important division had yet to be announced, that of Punjab, a rich province with a volatile mix of Sikhs, Muslims and Hindus. A decision had been made on Aug. 12, but Mountbatten had ordered its details unpublished until two days after India's independence. He foresaw chaos and wanted British responsibility for it to be moot by the time the screaming started over the new borders. No preparations were therefore made to control the inevitable havoc. The result was a bloody birthday gift to newborn India and Pakistan as millions of people were uprooted amid massacres and murder. "I am sick with horror," Nehru would write his friend Mountbatten after visiting one affected area. More horror was to come: refugee camps everywhere and, eventually, war with Pakistan over Kashmir, an enmity, potent as nuclear bombs, that lasts to this day. —*By Howard Chua-Eoan*

What TIME Said Then

In India and Pakistan since mid-August at least 100,000 have died, not of germs or hunger or what the law calls "acts of God," but of brutal slaughter. Everywhere the armed and the many devoured the helpless and the few. —*Oct. 27, 1947*

ON THE MOVE
Millions took to the road the day the country was divided

Aug. 15, 1947

Oct. 14, 1947

What TIME Said Then

So many airplanes had met disaster far below sonic speed that the "sonic wall" had earned a fearful reputation. Designers and pilots spoke of it with awe. It was widely believed that when an airplane reached the speed of sound, it would disintegrate. —*April 18, 1949*

Busting Through The Sound Barrier

Chuck Yeager's two cracked ribs hurt like hell, but he was darned if a little tumble from a horse in the Mojave Desert was going to stop him from breaking the sound barrier. The U.S. Air Force was counting on him. It was his ninth flight in the experimental rocket plane XS-1, each one having edged closer to Mach 1, the never crossed barrier past which man would fly faster than the speed of sound. It was dangerous, he knew. A British test pilot had been blown to bits going Mach 0.94. The crew at Murdoc Air Base in California, not knowing the extent of Yeager's injuries, sent him off with a jolly "Hi-yo, Silver!"

Climbing painfully down into the XS-1 as it lay in the airborne belly of the huge mother ship, a B-29, Yeager snapped the

A Pioneer's Bold Strokes

Jackson Pollock couldn't get to sleep. The next night would see the opening of the first gallery show devoted to his new drip paintings. For months he had flung lashing tangles of color onto canvases laid across the floor. Literally slapdash, yet as intricately woven as a Persian rug, his pictures pointed the way to the future—or would if anyone noticed. So Pollock sat up late with his sister-in-law. To comfort him, she read his palm. He was going to be a very famous painter, she promised him.

That may not have been evident at Betty Parson's Manhattan gallery, where Pollock watched the guests snort in puzzlement. Later came the reviews ("monotonous intensity"). The sales? Two canvases. But within the American avant-garde, a world consumed by disputes that consumed him too, the show was a loudly argued challenge. When the mostly skeptical mass media came around, the Abstract Expressionists, who had been germinating for years, exploded American art onto the world stage for the first time.

And Pollock? He was America's first painter–pop star, the drunken angel of an emerging hipster culture in search of new routes to those old American goals, the instinctive and the transcendent. Though the role unnerved him, it was secured forever in 1956, when he died, like James Dean, in a car crash. But by that time the energies he had released were in motion everywhere. The painter Willem de Kooning said it best: "He broke the ice." True enough, but it broke him too.

—By Richard Lacayo

cover shut using a sawed-off broom. At 20,000 ft., he dropped out of the bomb bay with a jolt. With all four rockets firing, the plane started shaking violently. The Mach needle edged up past 0.965, and then it went off the scale. Yeager was thunderstruck. He was flying supersonic, and "it was as smooth as a baby's bottom. Grandma could be sitting up there sipping lemonade," he said later. He half didn't believe it—until the tracking crew ran up and reported hearing the world's first sonic boom, a sound that marked the end of the Wright Brothers' era and the beginning of the age of the astronauts. His XS-1 had accelerated to Mach 1.06, or 700 m.p.h.

That night Yeager fixed his buddies a pitcher of martinis to celebrate. But the world would have to wait to learn of Yeager's feat. It was all top secret until *Aviation Week* broke the story in December. The government wouldn't come around to confirming it had happened until May 1948.

—By Cathy Booth Thomas

Jan. 5, 1948

POLLOCK: He flung paint—sometimes ordinary house paint— as he merged process with product

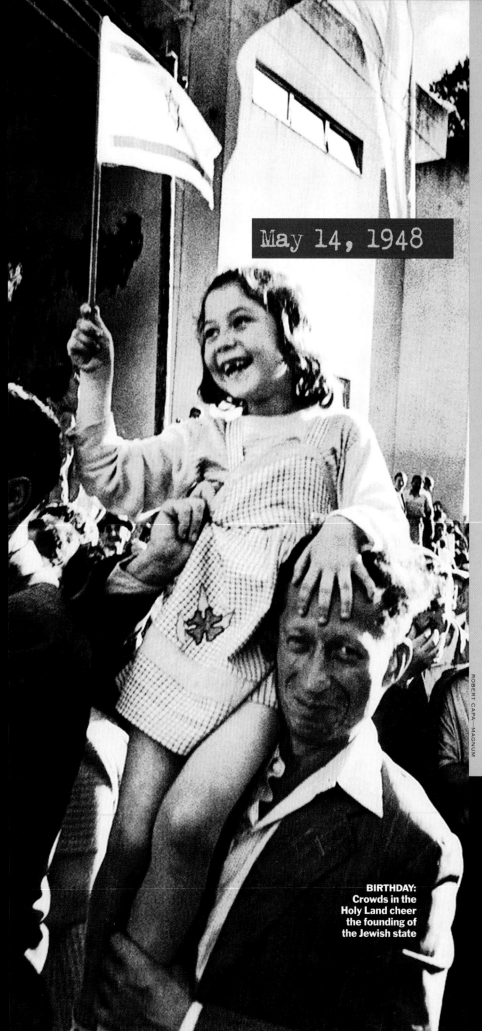

May 14, 1948

BIRTHDAY:
Crowds in the
Holy Land cheer
the founding of
the Jewish state

ROBERT CAPA—MAGNUM

Jews Give Birth To a New Nation

What I am trying to do is make the whole world safe for Jews," Harry Truman wrote as he wrestled over the decision to recognize a Jewish state in Palestine. Deeply affected by the Holocaust, Truman sympathized with Jewish aspirations for a homeland. In November 1947 he lobbied for the U.N. resolution that divided Palestine into Jewish and Arab states. Britain announced it would hand authority over Palestine to the U.N. by May 14, 1948. Secretary of State George Marshall advised against recognition, warning Truman that neighboring Arab countries would cut off oil and unite to destroy the Jews. On the eve of British withdrawal—to be followed by an immediate Jewish declaration of independence—he told Truman "the great office of the President" was at stake.

But Truman's mind was made up. At 4 p.m., David Ben-Gurion read a 979-word declaration of independence in front of a small audience at the Tel Aviv Art Museum. He finished, "The state of Israel is established! The meeting is ended." At midnight, British rule over Palestine lapsed; 11 minutes later White House spokesman Charlie Ross announced U.S. recognition. "God put you in your mother's womb," the Chief Rabbi of Israel later told Truman, "so you would be the instrument to bring the rebirth of Israel." With Truman's decision, the hopes of the Jewish people were realized, but so too were Marshall's fears. Arab opponents of the new nation immediately declared war, prompting a bloody struggle over Israel's existence that would rage into the next century. —*By Romesh Ratnesar*

What TIME Said Then

In the two hours that remained before sundown, when the Jewish Sabbath would begin, Tel Aviv's jubilant people danced in the streets, paraded with blue-and-white streamers and Star of David flags ... — *May 24, 1948*

RED-RIBBON DAY:
Mao declares the birth
of the communist
People's Republic

Oct. 1, 1949

Dawn of Mao's Marxist China

Mao Zedong inexplicably arrived an hour early at the red-lacquered Gate of Eternal Peace, the entrance to the 500-year-old palace of China's emperors. He had chosen a symbol of ancient power in which to declare his new China. The man in charge of preparations, a loyal soldier named Guo Ying, 24, who had been fighting with the communists since he was 13, seated Mao in the former emperor's waiting room and fetched him a bowl of apples. There Guo learned that Mao, in his haste, had forgotten the ribbon that each new communist leader pins to his tunic.

Just outside, in Tiananmen Square, 300,000 people squinted through a yellow haze of soot to see the man who, after two decades of fighting, had routed the American-backed forces of Generalissimo Chiang Kai-shek. As Mao waited, Guo dispatched a comrade to find a piece of red satin and write "chairman" upon it in gold. That crisis averted, Mao stood on the rostrum above a massive portrait of himself and announced in his peasant brogue, "The central government of the People's Republic of China is established!" "Long live Chairman Mao!" answered the crowd, which began cheering communist soldiers fresh from battle as they marched in the new country's first military parade. Guo stood behind Mao and wept for "a victory won with the blood of millions of revolutionaries."

—By Matthew Forney

BROWN BROTHERS

THOMAS D. MCAVOY—TIMEPIX

FRANKLIN ROOSEVELT AND WINSTON CHURCHILL Their first meeting—Aug. 9, 1941, off Newfoundland's coast— was secret. Its product: a set of "common principles" that came to be called the Atlantic Charter. The tide had turned: America had cast her lot with Britain

Fateful Meetings

BRANCH RICKEY AND JACKIE ROBINSON On Aug. 28, 1945, the Dodgers' top man challenged the speedy star: "You've got to do this job with base hits and stolen bases and fielding ground balls, Jackie. Nothing else." The reply: "Mr. Rickey, I've got two cheeks." After Robinson weathered a season in the minor leagues, the Dodgers had a new infielder

BETTMANN CORBIS

JUAN PERÓN AND EVA DUARTE The earth moved, and they met. On Jan. 15, 1944, an earthquake hit Argentina. At a benefit for victims, radio actress Duarte sidled up to Colonel Perón. The Lady had found her Macbeth. Perón was elected in 1946 and ran Argentina with Evita by his side until her death, at 33, from cancer in 1952

■ Karl Doenitz

When his U-boats sailed out to war, Doenitz was a Vice Admiral commanding the most effective underwater force in any navy. And he knew how to apply the force. He introduced wolf-pack tactics (*Rudeltaktik*) for attacking convoys. He varied this technique with individual sorties, sometimes into enemy ports or rivers. And he perfected a far-flung system of radio control, directing U-boats at sea from a central headquarters on land.

Doenitz knew the British well, and he had profound contempt for them at the war's start. In the last war, after service on a cruiser in the Mediterranean, he was transferred to U-boats, earned his own command. His UB-68 was sunk by the British off Malta in 1918. Rescued, Doenitz was taken to England as a prisoner of war. There he so successfully feigned mental illness that his captors kept him comfortably in a sanatorium.

His headquarters is a fantastic structure, designed to resemble a warship on land. His office has a few pieces of period furniture, a broad expanse of bookshelves filled with tomes on naval history. Scattered about are gaily colored, crude models of the ships which one of his U-boats sank on a successful cruise. On the wall behind him is a portrait of his revered predecessor, Grand Admiral Alfred von Tirpitz, who ardently advocated unrestricted U-boat warfare 26 years ago. **—May 10, 1943**

■ Joe Louis

Today, after four years of monopolizing the world's heavyweight championship, he is not only the idol of his race but one of the most respectable prize-fighters of all time. From the sorry pass to which a series of second-raters had brought it (Sharkey, Carnera, Baer, Braddock), he restored the world's championship to the gate and almost the vigor that it had in Jack Dempsey's day.

He did other notable things: he took on all comers, fought 20 times in four years, was never accused of a fixed fight, an unfair punch, a disparaging comment. All this did not make Joe Louis a dramatic figure but it stored up treasure in Heaven and on earth for Joe Louis and his people.
—Sept. 29, 1941

■ Bill Mauldin's "Willie"

Willie was born, full-grown, during the Italian campaign. He needed a shave and his clothes hung in weary folds on his weary frame. Even on his day of creation, his thick fingers were curved, as though from grasping a pick handle or an M-I rifle. He did not smile then and he has never smiled since.

Willie was born into the 45th Infantry Division, where his creator, Private Bill Mauldin, also served. Willie had a sidekick, Joe. Together Willie and Joe slogged from Italy to Germany. Willie and Joe were combat infantrymen. **—June 18, 1945**

■ Bob Hope

From the ranks of show business have sprung heroes and even martyrs, but so far only one legend. That legend is Bob Hope. It sprang up swiftly, telepathically, among U.S. servicemen in Britain this summer, traveling faster than even whirlwind Hope himself.

Hope was funny, treating hordes of soldiers to roars of laughter. He was friendly—ate with servicemen, drank with them, read their doggerel, listened to their songs. He was indefatigable, running himself ragged with five, six, seven shows a day. He was figurative—the straight link with home, the radio voice that for years had filled the living room. When he came, anonymous guys who had no other recognition felt personally remembered. **—Sept. 20, 1943**

APRIL 19, 1956 The daughter of a Philadelphia industrialist, Grace Kelly first conquered Hollywood, then won the heart of Prince Rainier III of Monaco. Their wedding capped the era's most celebrated romance

MAY 6, 1954 A young British medical student, Roger Bannister, was first to run the mile in under four minutes, clocking in at 3:59:04. His secret: "It's the art of taking more out of yourself than you've got"

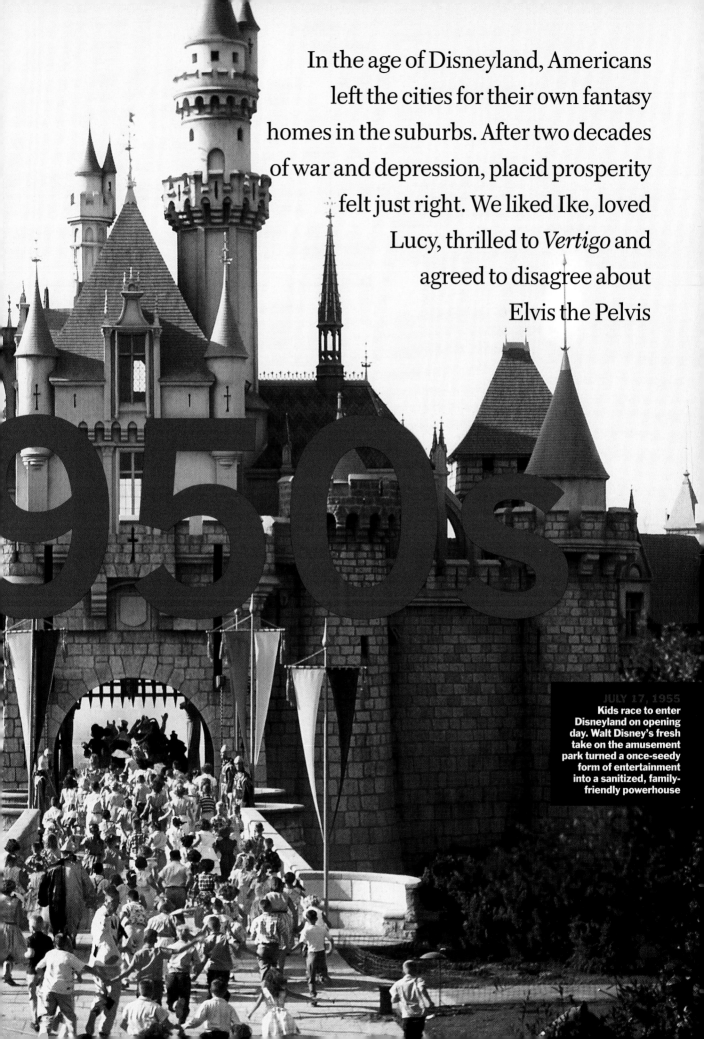

In the age of Disneyland, Americans left the cities for their own fantasy homes in the suburbs. After two decades of war and depression, placid prosperity felt just right. We liked Ike, loved Lucy, thrilled to *Vertigo* and agreed to disagree about Elvis the Pelvis

1950s

JULY 17, 1955
Kids race to enter Disneyland on opening day. Walt Disney's fresh take on the amusement park turned a once-seedy form of entertainment into a sanitized, family-friendly powerhouse

Feb. 9, 1950

McCarthy Delivers His First Slander

Joseph McCarthy was just an obscure backbench Senator from Wisconsin looking for a political edge when he arrived in Wheeling, W.Va., to address a Lincoln Day dinner. He wasn't even sure what he was going to say, so he took along a speech on federal housing programs and another on alleged communists in government. A local Republican advised that the commie speech would have more oomph. And so that night, McCarthy, waving a paper in the air, proclaimed, "I have here in my hand a list of 205 that were made known to the Secretary of State as being members of the Communist Party ..."

Overnight, his speech sparked a media firestorm that played to the basest fears of Americans swept up in a frightening cold war and triggered loyalty oaths, blacklists and

TIME OUT!
Murrow, right, and Flanders blew the whistle on McCarthy

AP/WIDE WORLD

JACK LARTZ—BETTMANN-CORBIS

BETTMANN-CORBIS

J'ACCUSE! McCarthy's 1950 speech touched off a four-year reign of terror in America

■ Crying Foul

During his four-year run as a demagogue, Joseph McCarthy always had virulent critics on the left. It wasn't until middle-of-the road Americans spoke out that his fear-mongering tactics began to pall. One of the first to condemn McCarthy was the revered CBS newsman, Edward R. Murrow. On his *See It Now* program on March 9, 1954, he said, "This is no time for men who oppose Senator McCarthy's methods to keep silent ... We can deny our heritage and our history, but we cannot escape responsibility for the result."

When a fellow G.O.P. Senator, Vermont's respected Ralph Flanders, rebuked McCarthy and introduced a resolution of censure in the Senate in July 1954, support for the Wisconsin Senator quickly evaporated.

personal betrayals that cost an estimated 10,000 Americans their jobs and some shattered innocents their lives. In 1954 he turned his bullying on the U.S. Army in widely watched television hearings that ultimately exposed McCarthy for the fraudulent demagogue he was. He died a broken alcoholic three years later, but his name remains synonymous with the most reviled style of American politics. **—By Johanna McGeary**

What TIME Said Then

Like a desperate gambler, McCarthy was doubling his bet every time he took a loss ... [now he] produced the most tremendous sensation yet. He would name a man "now connected" with the State Department who was "the top Russian espionage agent in the U.S." *—April 3, 1950*

Falling in Love with Lucy

The evening that *I Love Lucy* first went on the air, the director and his wife invited us all to have dinner and watch the premiere. Lucy and Desi were there, along with producer Jess Oppenheimer and his wife, Vivian Vance and her husband, and our editor, Dann Cahn. We gathered around the 12-in. screen to watch the opening episode, "The Girls Want to Go to a Nightclub." We had seen the show at the filming, so there wasn't much laughter. But Vivian's husband Phil Ober, who hadn't been at the filming, was laughing so hard he almost fell out of his chair, which we hoped was a good omen.

When the reviews appeared, they were mixed. The *Hollywood Reporter* gave it a rave. *Daily Variety* said the show needed work, but the New York *Times* thought it had "promise." TIME called it "a triumph of bounce over bumbling material." When the ratings came out, *I Love Lucy* was in the Top 10, and six months later it reached No. 1. People ask why the show was an immediate hit and has remained popular for more than 50 years. Most of the credit goes to the incredible comedy genius of Lucille Ball.

I Love Lucy established a lot of records. It has been seen by more than 1 billion people. But one of the show's biggest contributions to TV was something that happened before we ever went on the air. In the early '50s, most TV shows were performed for live broadcast in New York City, and stations around the country played a kinescope, a copy of the show filmed from a TV screen, which wasn't of good quality. But Lucy and Desi were expecting their first child, and they didn't want to move to New York. So Desi got a group of top technical people together who figured out how to shoot the show with three film cameras in front of an audience. CBS said that would cost too much, so Desi and Lucy took a cut in salary and in return were given the rights to the negatives of the films. Thus the three-camera film system, still used for situation comedies today, was created, and the rerun was born.

—By Madelyn Pugh Davis and Bob Carroll

Davis and Carroll co-wrote the pilot for I Love Lucy *and stayed with the show for six years.*

What TIME Said Then

Lucille Ball romps engagingly through a series of vaudeville routines, gets adequate assistance from her husband, Cuban bandleader/singer Desi Arnaz, and raucous support from William Frawley and Vivian Vance. —*Nov. 12, 1951*

■ Lucy's Litter

The sitcom format pioneered by Desi Arnaz and Lucille Ball has proved infinitely adaptable, holding up the mirror to decades of social change in U.S. families—and even in faux families like *Seinfeld*'s Gang of Four.

Ozzie & Harriet The four Nelsons played themselves—but that was as real as this 1952 hit got. Following the '50s formula, it portrayed an idealized, sanitized, all-American family

All in the Family Producer Norman Lear used his 1971 show as a lance, skewering racial bigotry and social hypocrisy while limning the growing division between U.S. generations

The Osbournes Egad! Lucy and Desi were never like this—but beneath the expletives deleted and memories of substance abuse past, MTV's 2002 hit presents a loving, functioning (if multiply pierced) family

The Cosby Show *I Love Lucy* updated to the 1980s, it broke precedent simply by bringing a "normal" black family into U.S. living rooms

Oct. 15, 1951

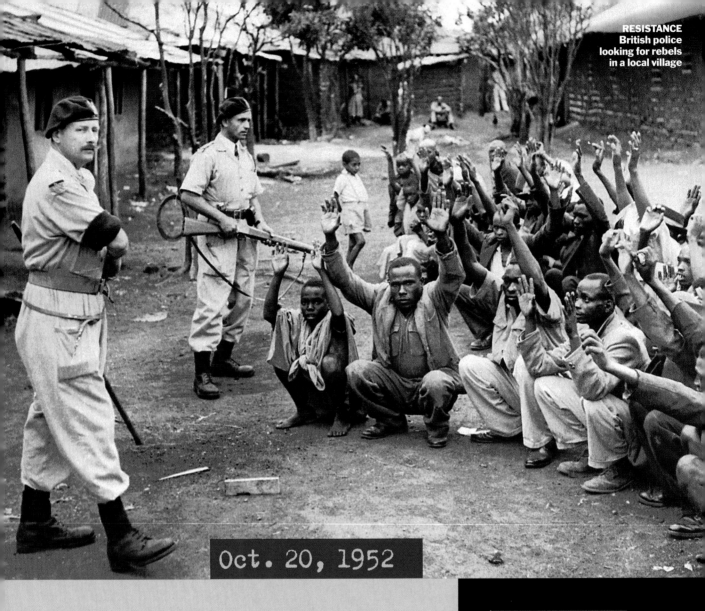

Oct. 20, 1952

The Bloody Mau Mau Revolt

What TIME Said Then

Part land hunger, part savage revolution against the domineering white man and the bewildering 20th century, the ...Mau Mau have already mutilated scores of whites and "loyal" blacks, with their favorite weapon, the panga—a long, machete-like knife. —*Nov. 3, 1952*

Chief Kungu Waruhiu had just arrived at the Seventh-Day Adventist mission seven miles outside of Nairobi when a fusillade of shots smashed into his car, killing the Kikuyu leader instantly. The gunmen were Mau Mau rebels, members of a secret society who had vowed to drive the white man from the British colony of Kenya.

The Mau Mau were already accused of a series of arson and cattle-killing incidents, and the dramatic daylight assassination of a prominent British loyalist from their own tribe stunned the colonial government into calling a state of emergency that lasted nearly eight years. British troops were brought in. More than 100,000 Africans were put into detention camps. The killings continued, and news reports about the Mau Mau's bloody massacres of white settlers living in the highlands of central Kenya horrified the world. In fact, only 32 Europeans died in the uprising, while almost 2,000 Kikuyu loyal to the British crown were murdered before the colonial government was finally able to regain control.

The turn to violence by the Mau Mau in Kenya emboldened independence movements across Africa, frustrated with years of broken promises on land reform and self-government. After a largely nonviolent political process, Ghana was the first former colony to win its freedom, in 1957. Kenya would have to wait another six years for freedom.

—By Marguerite Michaels

Deciphering the Double Helix

James Watson remembers cringing when his colleague Francis Crick announced to regulars at the Eagle, a pub in Cambridge, England, that they had discovered "the secret of life." True, the onetime ornithologist and the former physicist had created a plausible model for the structure of DNA that morning. If they were right, biologists would finally understand how parents pass characteristics on to their children—not only hair and eye color but every aspect of how the human body is built and how it operates. Watson, an American, and Crick, a Briton, would have solved the mysteries of heredity and of evolution, all in one shot.

But they also might have been wrong, as they had been a year and a half earlier,

when the two rookies had made some dumb mistakes. Even Linus Pauling, the world's greatest chemist, had blown his own "solution" to DNA a couple of months before. So while their double-helix model seemed to make biochemical sense and agreed with what was already known, a wiser man might have toned down his rhetoric.

The fact that double helix and Watson and Crick are familiar to just about every schoolchild, though, makes it clear that DNA was every bit as important as Crick thought. Not only did it explain heredity, but it would also lead to such practical applications as DNA forensics in law enforcement, testing for genetic diseases and the development of an entire biotechnology industry. With the recent completion of the Human Genome Project, it could radically change the way medicine is practiced over the next few decades. Crick's bold assertion was, if anything, stunningly accurate.

—By Michael Lemonick

TWISTED
Watson, left, and Crick examine their first model of the double helix

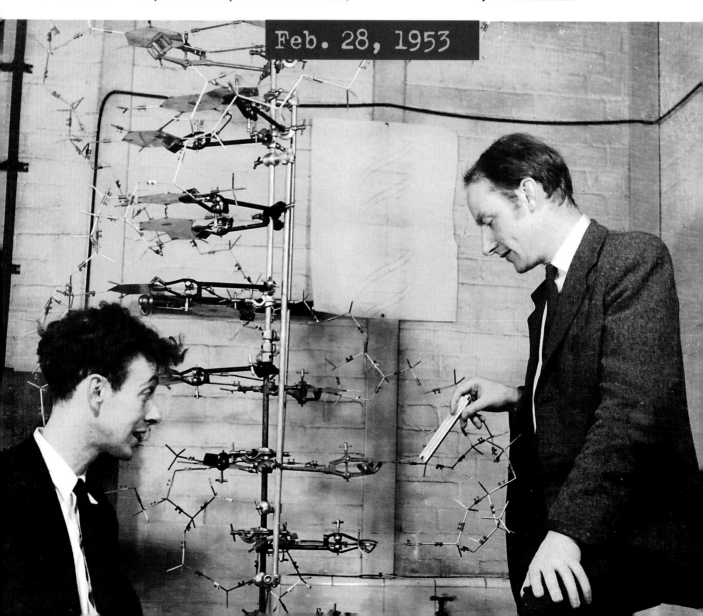

Feb. 28, 1953

FIRST NOTES Elvis takes a break during a recording session in the Sun Records studio

July 5, 1954

The King Finds His Voice

It was only an audition. That's why there were no drums, no backup singers and no expectations. Sam Phillips had heard about a good-looking local kid who favored ballads, knew a few guitar chords and was blessed with the ostentatiously original name Elvis Presley. In his search for a new sound, Phillips had run nearly every singer in Memphis through his Sun Records studio; on that Monday summer evening, Elvis, 19, was merely next in line.

Phillips asked two trusted session musicians—guitarist Scotty Moore and bassist Bill Black—to provide backup, and at 7 p.m., after a few minutes of small talk and nervous laughter, Phillips arranged the trio in a circle. Then he asked Elvis what he wanted to play. There was more nervous laughter; Elvis knew only a few songs, and most of those he couldn't play from start to finish. Somehow, the group fumbled through the mawkish *Harbor Lights*, which had been a 1950 hit for Bing Crosby. From the control room, Phillips drawled, "That's pretty good," although it wasn't. Elvis sounded boring, mechanical. Phillips called a break.

With the formalities suspended, Elvis picked up a guitar and started goofing around, playing an old blues song by Arthur (Big Boy) Crudup, *That's All Right*. Except Elvis wasn't singing the blues. He sounded almost euphoric, and the rhythm was off—far too frenetic. There were no drums, so Black was slapping his bass to keep time while Moore's guitar leaped in and out of the melody line. Phillips knew immediately. He stuck his head out of the control room and told the threesome to pick a place to start and keep playing. Two nights later, *That's All Right* was played on Memphis radio, and the era of rock 'n' roll roared into life. —*By Josh Tyrangiel*

■ Sam's Ears of Gold

Without producer Sam Phillips, there may have been no Elvis Presley phenomenon. The Florence, Ala., native, who turned 80 in 2003, was present at the creation of a host of legendary musical careers. The sheer roll call of the geniuses who passed through his studio reads like an

MAN BEHIND THE GLASS: Phillips, right, with Elvis, Bill Black and Scotty Moore in 1954

encyclopedia entry on blues, rockabilly and rock 'n' roll: B.B. King, Howlin' Wolf, Carl Perkins, Johnny Cash, Jerry Lee Lewis, Roy Orbison, Charlie Rich.

Phillips' genius was to focus his artists on the type of sound that best suited their talents. In Elvis' case, this meant homing in on up-tempo numbers rather than treacly ballads. As Peter Guralnick, writer of the mammoth Presley biography, told the Los Angeles *Times* in 2000, "Sam was the person who, purely on the basis of instinct, waited Elvis out in the studio while he sang all kinds of things which may have been pretty, but were nowhere close to the direction that people have come to recognize as Elvis Presley's music."

What TIME Said Then

His entire body takes on a frantic quiver, as if he had swallowed a jackhammer. Full-cut hair tousles over his forehead, and sideburns frame his petulant, full-lipped face ... the sight and sound of him drive teenage girls wild. —*May 14, 1956*

VICTORY LAP:
Jesse Jackson hails
Rosa Parks at the
Democratic National
Convention, 1988

BILL PIERCE (TOP); AP/WIDE WORLD (RIGHT).

■ A Legend's Later Years

When Rosa Parks stood up for her right to sit down in 1955, she was 42 years old. Today she is a hale, much-loved American icon of 90. Not by nature a public figure, she has begun in recent years to accept the honors and plaudits of other Americans, who realize that she represents a heroic age of social progress whose key figures are beginning to pass from the scene.

Douglas Brinkley's 2000 biography, *Rosa Parks,* and a 2002 CBS drama, *The Rosa Parks Story,* starring Angela Bassett, introduced Parks' story to a new generation of Americans. Indeed, the lionization of Parks has become so pervasive that it provoked a backlash: the 2002 comedy *Barbershop* dared to lampoon her, provoking a national outcry—and her own displeasure. Perhaps a better estimate of her significance to U.S. society was made by the Henry Ford Museum in Dearborn, Mich.: in 2001, it paid $492,000 to buy the Montgomery city bus in which Parks refused to budge on that famous occasion.

And as for that momentous event: here is a little historical revisionism from one who was there. "People always say that I didn't give up my seat because I was tired, but that isn't true," Parks wrote in her 1991 autobiography, *Rosa Parks: My Story.* "The only tired I was, was tired of giving in."

PAYING THE PRICE:
Parks is fingerprinted two
months after refusing
to give up her seat

What TIME Said Then

Overnight the word flashed throughout the various Negro neighborhoods: support Rosa Parks; don't ride the buses Monday. Within 48 hours mimeo-graphed leaflets were out, calling for a one-day bus boycott. On Monday Montomery Negroes walked, rode mules, drove horse-drawn buggies, traveled to work in private cars. — *Feb. 18, 1957*

Rosa Parks had just worked a hard day as a seamstress in the basement of the Montgomery Fair department store in Montgomery, Ala., and she had to run a youth-group meeting later that night for her local N.A.A.C.P., which had been trying to find a way to protest the city's segregation laws. Still, Parks didn't get right on the bus when she left work that Thursday evening. The bus stop was crowded, so she headed to a drugstore to shop

Dec. 1, 1955

A Bus Rider's Defiance

for an electric heating pad, thinking she would be able to get a seat home if she waited a bit. When she finally deposited her 10¢ fare on the Cleveland Avenue bus, she found a seat in the first row of the "colored" section in the back. But after a few stops, the driver ordered her to get up so a white passenger could sit down. Parks refused, and the police were called to take her to jail. Two hours after her arrest, she was released on $100 bail. By midnight, a plan had been hatched for a citywide bus boycott, which a young Baptist minister named Martin Luther King Jr. would later be elected to direct. The boycott lasted 381 days, until the Supreme Court ruled that segregation on buses was illegal; its success ignited the modern civil rights movement. "When I declined to give up my seat, it was not that day or bus in particular," Parks later told her biographer Douglas Brinkley. "I just wanted to be free, like everybody else." **—By Anita Hamilton**

SKYWARD
The Soviets launch the basketball-size Sputnik, below

Oct. 4, 1957

RIA NOVOSTI (2)

An Unforeseen Orbiter Ignites the Space Race

Some 50 scientists from 13 countries, all members of the International Geophysical Year's conference on rockets and satellites, had gathered, along with a handful of journalists, for cocktails that night at the Soviet embassy on Washington's 16th Street. New York *Times* science reporter Walter Sullivan was called to the phone and told that Moscow had announced that it had put a satellite into orbit. He hurried back and whispered the news in the ear of U.S. physicist Lloyd Berkner, who rapped on the hors d'oeuvre table until the hubbub quieted and dramatically declared to the unknowing and startled group, including the Russians, "A satellite is in orbit at an elevation of 900 km. I wish to congratulate our Soviet colleagues on their achievement."

Washington changed in those next few hours. The U.S., which had assumed scientific pre-eminence, had been beaten in the opening lap of the space race. Before the night was over the Russians had fueled themselves with vodka and stood curbside in front of their embassy, staring into the night sky, singing and cheering.

I didn't go to bed that night, rushing from the Soviet embassy to Capitol Hill to the White House. Those at the center of the power game knew their lives had changed. At the Naval Research Laboratory, which was in charge of America's entry in the space race, Project Vanguard, the engineers bathed the roof in searchlights so they could adjust their radio dishes to pick up the defiant beep from Sputnik, the 184-lb. intruder that had not only humiliated the U.S. but ratcheted up the cold war. The Soviet rockets obviously were bigger and better than we knew.

The White House feigned indifference and reassured the nation about American scientific prowess. But worry seeped through the nation, always uncomfortable with second place. When the U.S. hurried its thin, finely engineered rocket, with a satellite, to the launching pad two months later, Vanguard lurched, buckled and blew up on the ground. The gentle astronomer John Hagen, who headed Project Vanguard, sucked on his ever present pipe and rightly pointed out that U.S. space science was more sophisticated than that of the Soviets. But by then the game had moved beyond pure science. Two young and driven politicians took notice. Senate majority leader Lyndon Johnson seized the moment of doubt and pushed the U.S. space program forward in Congress. Senator John Kennedy saw space as the next great national adventure, and when he became President four years later, he decided to land Americans on the moon. **—By Hugh Sidey**

What TIME Said Then

Over thousands of earthbound radios came the eerie *beep ... beep ... beep* from somewhere out in space. In the nation's reaction to those chilling beeps, the impulse to applaud a mighty scientific achievement soon froze in the rigors of the cold war. *—Oct. 14, 1957*

UNBURIED TREASURE:
Mary and Louis Leakey
examine fossils they
found in Tanzania

July 17, 1959

Uncovering Earliest Man

My father was ill that morning, so my mother set out alone in the Land Rover, accompanied by her two Dalmatians, Sally and Victoria. She spent the morning crawling along the slope of the nearby gorge but found very little until just before noon, when she noticed a scrap of enormously thick bone protruding from beneath the surface. She instantly realized that it was part of a hominid skull—and that two teeth were embedded in the rock just above it. Elated, she drove back to camp to tell my father Louis. As he remembered it, she rushed in crying, "I've got him! I've got him! I've got him!"

What my mother Mary had discovered was the fragments of a fossil skull that was later to be named *Zinjanthropus boisei*. The find was to rivet world attention on the Olduvai Gorge in Tanganyika (now Tanzania) and on the work of my parents.

I arrived at Olduvai a day after the skull was found. My parents' simple camp seemed to radiate the excitement of the moment, and I don't recall ever seeing my parents in such high spirits. The skull that my mother recovered was in many pieces, but she and my father were able to piece it back together. It was the first really significant find at Olduvai; indeed, it was the only well-preserved fossil hominid to have been found outside South Africa, several thousand miles to the south. Unlike the South African sites, which lacked distinct geological layers, Olduvai offered a chance to get some real ages for the fossils. Using a method known as potas-sium-argon dating, *Zinjanthropus* was determined to be 1.75 million years old. At the time, this was staggering. It almost tripled the skull's estimated age, which had been obtained by geological interpretation. It stretched back our evolutionary perspective.

Since that day, hundreds of hominid fossils have been discovered across a wide range of African sites. Many of these are undoubtedly of greater scientific interest than the 1959 find, but in my opinion no other discovery has had the impact on this field of human inquiry. The dating of the Olduvai strata began a new chapter in our understanding of human origins: it added the dimension of real time to evolution.

—**By Richard Leakey**

Leakey, now an environmentalist, is working on an international wildlife-conservation fund for East Africa.

AP/WORLD WIDE

FIDEL CASTRO AND CHE GUEVARA
Argentine doctor Guevara and Cuban lawyer Castro crossed paths at a friend's house in Mexico in July 1955. The privileged pair had much in common: a hatred of the U.S. influence on Latin America and a belief that guerrilla action could liberate the masses. It worked: on New Year's Day in 1959, the two rebels took power in Cuba

Fateful Meetings

JOHN LENNON AND PAUL McCARTNEY
Lennon's band, the Quarry Men, was setting up to play a dance on July 6, 1957, when a 15-year-old bloke grabbed a guitar and ripped through two rockabilly tunes. Lennon was wary of sharing leadership, but admiration won the day, and the Beatles' core had come together

APPLE

EDMUND HILLARY AND TENZING NORGAY
Hillary was a New Zealand beekeeper; Tenzing Norgay a Nepalese porter. Paired up as the fastest team on a British expedition to conquer Mount Everest, they set off in the predawn hours of May 29, 1953. At 11:30 a.m., they spiked their names in the snows of history

Snapshots

■ Leonard Bernstein

In an age of specialization, he refuses to stay put in any cultural pigeon-hole. He is a Mickey Mantle of music, a brilliant switch hitter, conducting with his right hand and composing with his left—not to mention several other occupations that would be full-time careers for other men. His extraordinary gyrations have earned him a reputation in some circles as the Presley of the Podium. **—Feb. 4, 1957**

■ Grandma Moses

A sizable audience gathered to hear her talk about painting. Instead, she told them in detail how she made preserves, and concluded her talk by opening her handbag and showing a few samples. **—Dec. 28, 1953**

■ Matthew Ridgway

A few weeks after he took over, the Pentagon decided to convert the 82nd into one of the first U.S. airborne divisions. To show his men what paratrooping might be like, Ridgway, who had no particular airborne qualifications, hied himself to Fort Benning to make a parachute jump. "It was the most glorious feeling in the world," he told the dubious infantrymen ...

A fellow officer says: "It makes him personally offended to be shot at." In Normandy, Ridgway and an aide were surprised by a German tank which rumbled up from the rear. The aide dived into a hole. Ridgway whipped his rifle to his shoulder and fired. For some inexplicable reason, the tank turned and clanked away. "I got him," bellowed Ridgway. **—March 5, 1951**

■ Fulton J. Sheen

Bishop Sheen is a unique product of two unique historic forces—the Roman Catholic Church and the United States of America. Into the making of Fulton Sheen went St. Paul and Thomas Jefferson, Savonarola and George F. Babbitt.

Sheen is a dedicated man of God; he is also a go-getter. He can be truly moving as well as thoroughly corny. He can write a learned treatise on theology as well as a snappy fund-raising plug. He tries to guide man toward the City of God, but he is a well-known figure in the City of Man. **—April 14, 1952**

■ Casey Stengel

He was still the elder statesman of the national game, a grey-haired philosopher given to anarchic grammar and startling *non sequiturs*. When the spirit moved him, he was still the racy raconteur and acrobatic vaudevillian who could have panicked the Palace. He was also the best manager in the majors.

As a bushleaguer, he was already a clown. He wore loud ties with his baseball uniform and he insisted on practicing sliding while he trotted to his outfield post. "There was a lunatic asylum across from the centerfield fence. Them guys in the loony bin always cheered when they saw me slide. But my manager used to tap his forehead and say, 'It's only a matter of time, Stengel.'" **—Oct. 3, 1955**

1960s

NOV. 13, 1961
Cellist Pablo Casals plays at a dinner at the glittering Kennedy White House. It was a homecoming: Casals played for President Theodore Roosevelt in 1904

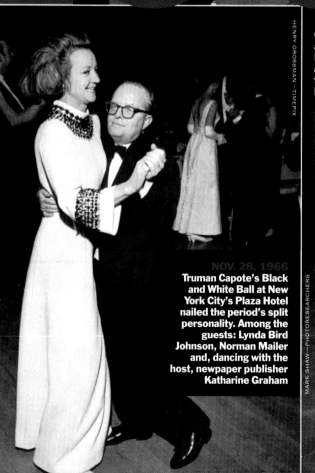

NOV. 28, 1966
Truman Capote's Black and White Ball at New York City's Plaza Hotel nailed the period's split personality. Among the guests: Lynda Bird Johnson, Norman Mailer and, dancing with the host, newpaper publisher Katharine Graham

In an era of discord and dichotomy, everyone took sides. White tie or tie-dye … classical or rock … young or old … Apollo or Dionysus … hawk or dove … choose now! In an amped-up age, the highs were higher, the lows lower, the frontiers newer, the skirts shorter and the hair longer

May 9, 1960

The Pill That Freed Sex

Margaret Sanger, totally unaware that her lifelong dream had become reality, spent the day at her home outside Tucson, Ariz. Since 1914 she had battled ridicule and rigid laws, even gone to jail, all in pursuit of a simple, inexpensive contraceptive that would change women's lives—and save some as well. Now she was 80 and retired from her globe-trotting efforts. No one from G.D. Searle & Co., the drug firm, thought to call the woman who had pioneered and pushed for funding to develop the world's first birth-control pill, called

Enovid-10, a synthetic combination of hormones that suppresses the release of eggs from a woman's ovaries. Nor did she hear from John Rock and Gregory Pincus, the doctors who developed the oral contraceptive with $3 million that Sanger had raised from her friend Katherine McCormick, the International Harvester heir.

Sanger got the news the next morning when her son Stuart and granddaughter Margaret read the newspaper. There they found a five-paragraph story announcing the Food and Drug Administration's approval of the pill as safe for birth control. The two, who lived next door, ran across the yard and opened the sliding glass door to Sanger's bedroom. It was 7 a.m., and she was eating breakfast in bed. Without the least

REVOLUTIONARIES:
Sanger crusading for
birth control in 1916.
Below, Gregory Pincus
holds the little wonder

Planting the Seeds
Of a Greener World

E xcerpted in the *New Yorker* three months before
it was published as a book, biologist Rachel
Carson's eloquent, rigorous attack on the
overuse of DDT and other pesticides—she called
them "elixirs of death"—had already upset the
chemical industry. Velsicol, maker of two top bug
killers, threatened to sue the book's publisher,

NATURE'S AIDE:
Carson at her
summer home
in Maine

Sept. 27, 1962

Houghton Mifflin, which stood firm but asked a toxi-
cologist to recheck Carson's facts before it shipped
Silent Spring to bookstores.

Carson spent publication day in her home in Silver
Spring, Md., preparing for speeches and a book tour, according to biographer Linda Lear. In a letter to a friend,
Carson called *Silent Spring* "something I believed in
so deeply that there was no other course; nothing that
ever happened made me even consider turning back."
When the book appeared, industry critics assailed
"the hysterical woman," but it became an instant best
seller with lasting impact. It spurred the banning of
DDT in the U.S., the passage of major environmental
laws and eventually a global treaty to phase out 12 pesticides known as "the dirty dozen." Carson died, at 56,
of cancer less than two years after the book's publication, but if she were alive today, she would undoubtedly warn about hundreds of other chemicals still released recklessly into nature.   —*By Charles Alexander*

bit of elation, just a sigh of relief, Sanger said,
"It's certainly about time." Then perking up,
she added, "Perhaps this calls for champagne."
Her son, a doctor who had patients waiting,
and her granddaughter, due for class at nurs-
ing school, begged off. So Margaret Sanger,
who had made a lifelong crusade of birth control after seeing her mother die at age 50,
worn out by 18 pregnancies and 11 children,
celebrated her victory alone—but triumphant.
    —*By Cathy Booth Thomas*

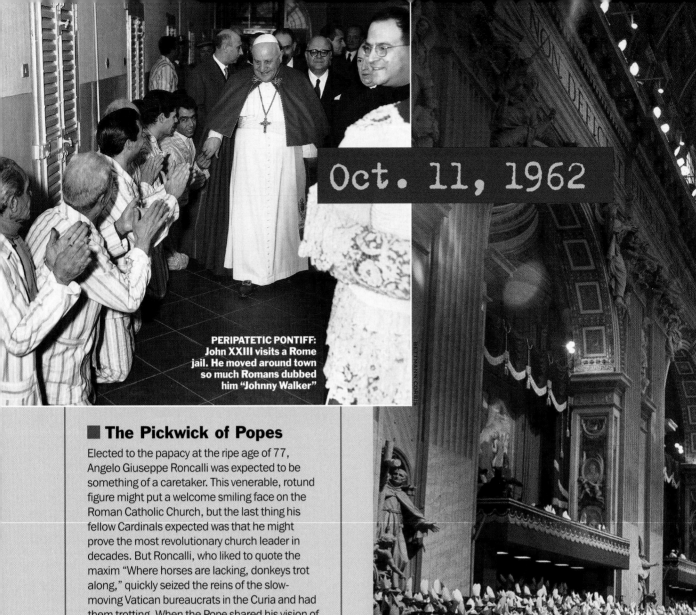

Oct. 11, 1962

PERIPATETIC PONTIFF: John XXIII visits a Rome jail. He moved around town so much Romans dubbed him "Johnny Walker"

■ The Pickwick of Popes

Elected to the papacy at the ripe age of 77, Angelo Giuseppe Roncalli was expected to be something of a caretaker. This venerable, rotund figure might put a welcome smiling face on the Roman Catholic Church, but the last thing his fellow Cardinals expected was that he might prove the most revolutionary church leader in decades. But Roncalli, who liked to quote the maxim "Where horses are lacking, donkeys trot along," quickly seized the reins of the slow-moving Vatican bureaucrats in the Curia and had them trotting. When the Pope shared his vision of holding a Vatican Council with his advisers, he was told, "We can't possibly get a council ready for 1963." "All right," he replied, "we'll have it in 1962."

Yet if John XXIII remains a beloved figure today, it is as much for his character as his council. His predecessor, Pius XII, was a frosty pillar of sanctity, a man who seemed to lack a human bloodstream, much less a human touch. The roly-poly Roncalli, born to a peasant family in Lombardy, was a lovable, beaming figure—the Pontiff as Mr. Pickwick—who once confided he was embarrassed to be referred to as "Holy Father." Just as he threw open the windows of the church in his council, he let sunlight in on the papacy, escaping the confines of the Vatican to visit Rome's local homes, parishes and prisons. Breaking through walls of suspicion, he espoused ecumenism and embraced leaders from a host of other religions. In sum, John XXIII took an insular, defensive, entrenched church and made it less Roman and more catholic.

A Church Transformed

They marched six abreast across the great square like some damask-clad, miter-capped army, the Cardinals in scarlet bringing up the rear. More than 2,600 bishops, the largest such gathering in the history of the Roman Catholic Church, took seats on 330-ft.-long bleachers in St. Peter's Basilica and craned like schoolboys for a view of the farmer's son who had called them here to . . . talk. About what? "About everything," one prelate predicted. "And a few things besides."

Angelo Giuseppe Roncalli, Pope John XXIII, put on his steel-rimmed spectacles and spoke for 38 minutes, after which his invitees went on for three more years. John died after the first session of the Second Vatican Council, but his ideal of the church's *aggiornamento,* or updating, flowered in unforeseen ways. By the council's end, the bishops turned the priest toward his flock during Mass and allowed its celebration in local languages, concluded it was not the Jews who killed Jesus, and in 16 hotly debated documents wrestled an all-too-medieval institution toward modernity.

The wrestling goes on. But on that first afternoon, John talked of the council's "beginning to rise in the church like the daybreak, the forerunner of the most splendid light." And the dawn was indeed inspiring, even if full illumination still tarries. ***—By David Van Biema***

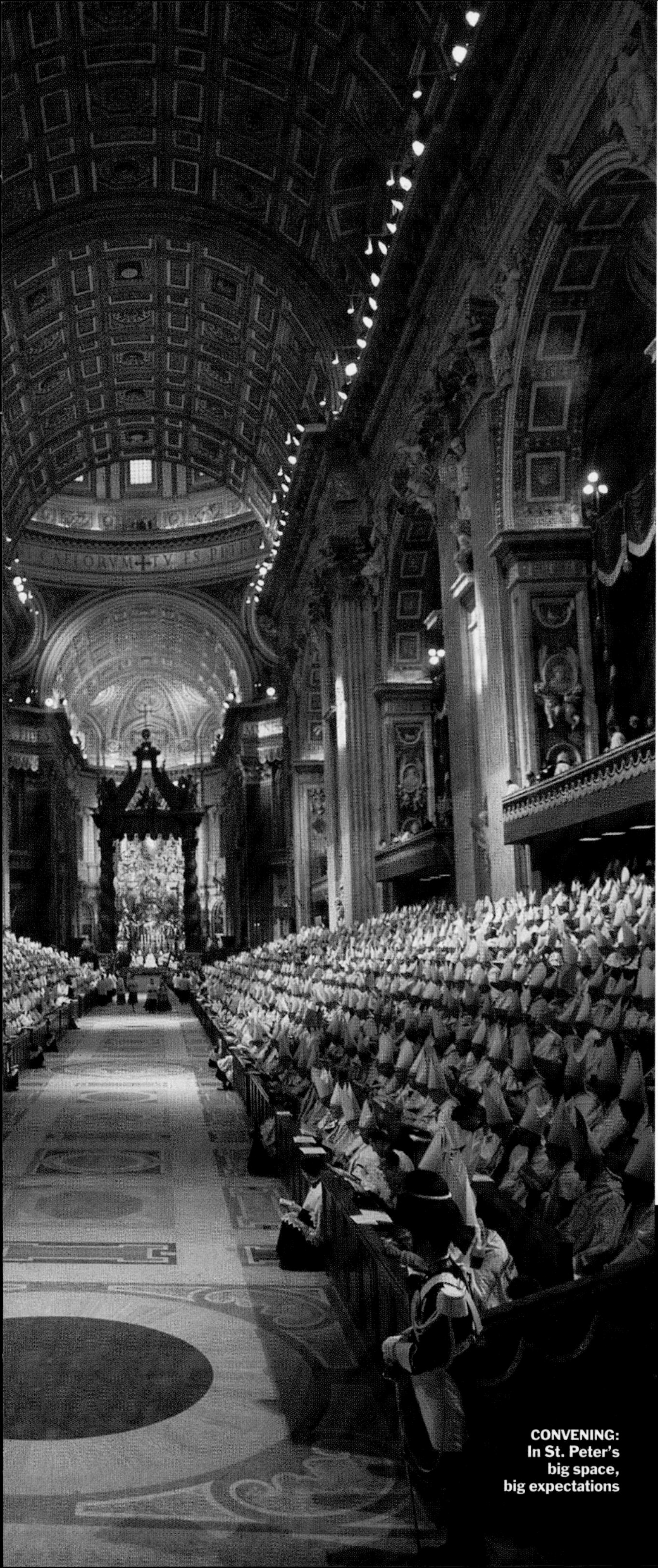

HANK WALKER—TIMEPIX

CONVENING: In St. Peter's big space, big expectations

What TIME Said Then

When the non-Catholic Christian observers to the Council gathered in the Sistine Chapel . . . they heard a significant departure from form: the Pontiff pointedly referred to himself in the first person singular, and spoke with moving humility. *—Oct. 26, 1962*

Averting the Apocalypse, by a Hair

A t 4 p.m., the Joint Chiefs recommended to President John F. Kennedy that the U.S. attack Cuba within 36 hours and destroy the Soviet missiles we had detected, believing—as the CIA estimated—the nuclear warheads had not yet been delivered. It would be a huge attack: the first day's air strike would be 1,080 sorties. This would be followed by an invasion; we had 180,000 troops mobilized in southeastern U.S. ports. We didn't learn until 30 years later that the Soviets already had 162 warheads in Cuba, and Fidel Castro had already recommended to Nikita Khrushchev that nuclear weapons be used if the U.S. invaded. That's how close we came. Events were slipping out of control.

When Kennedy first learned of the missiles, on Oct. 16, he knew he had to get them out of Cuba. For a month before, Soviet officials had told us no missiles had been delivered to Cuba and none would be. Clearly the Soviets had introduced them under the cloak of deception, and if they got away with that, they might believe they could do it elsewhere. That day Kennedy brought together his top advisers and told us to meet until we came to an agreement on what course to take.

By Oct. 21 there were two views: one group of advisers thought we should try to force the missiles out without military action, that is by a quarantine—we called it a quarantine because a blockade is an act of war—and the other group recommended an attack. Kennedy asked General Walter Sweeney, chief of the Tactical Air Command, if he was certain he could take out all the missiles. Sweeney replied, "We have the finest fighter force in the world; we have trained for this kind of operation, and they would destroy the great majority. But there might be one or two or five left." What President would knowingly take the risk of exposing millions of Americans to attack by not destroying

Oct. 27, 1962

CHERRY PICKER

LAUNCH PAD WITH ERECTOR

LAUNCH PAD WITH ERECTOR

MISSILE READY BLDGS

CABLING

FUELING VEHICLES

AT THE BRINK: J.F.K. announces the quarantine of Cuba, with U.S. troops ready to attack

HULTON ARCHIVE/GETTY IMAGES; DEPARTMENT OF DEFENSE (TOP)

one, two or five nuclear weapons? At that moment I knew Kennedy would decide on a quarantine.

Even so, by Oct. 27 Khrushchev was not giving any sign of backing down. We met all day with the President, split between those who believed we should attack and those who thought we should negotiate. The Joint Chiefs pushed for an invasion. Khrushchev had sent a hard-line offer that morning. But Kennedy decided simply to take the Soviet leader up on his offer of the previous night, proposing to withdraw the missiles if the U.S. promised not to invade Cuba. Khrushchev accepted on Sunday. He was so worried that war would break out in the six hours it took to encode and transmit a message from the Kremlin to the White House, he broadcast his response on Moscow public radio.

—By Robert McNamara

McNamara was J.F.K.'s Secretary of Defense.

■ A Nuclear Surprise

U.S. ambassador to the United Nations Adlai Stevenson shocked the world in October 1962 when he showed the Security Council aerial reconnaissance photos that clearly revealed Soviet troops in Cuba building bases for missiles that could reach nearby America. But it was not until 30 years later, as Robert McNamara notes in his account at left, that Americans first learned that at the time of the crisis, U.S. intelligence agencies had actually underestimated the extent of the threat.

In January 1992, some 20 former adversaries—senior U.S., former Soviet and Cuban officials—met in Havana to review those fateful days. After meeting with the generals, participant McNamara said, "We were told by the Russians that the Soviet forces in Cuba in October 1962—numbering 42,000 men, instead of the 10,000 reported by the CIA—possessed 36 nuclear warheads for the 24 intermediate-range missiles that were capable of striking the United States." It was the first time that the presence of Soviet nuclear warheads in Cuba had been made public.

What TIME Said Then

Khrushchev had sized up Kennedy as a weakling, given to strong talk and timorous action ... Kennedy shattered those illusions. He did it with a series of dramatic decisions that brought ... a showdown not with Fidel Castro but with Khrushchev's own Soviet Union —*Nov. 2, 1962*

LEWIS: The onetime rebel is now a Congressman

BOB ADELMAN—MAGNUM (KING); AP/WIDE WORLD (LEWIS)

■ Splinters and Dreams

As with all historic eras, the story of the civil rights movement is being radically simplified as it evolves from journalism into history. No one is likely to forget the legacy of the Rev. Martin Luther King Jr., yet he was just one man in the mighty army that marched for equality. One of King's closest associates, John Lewis, can still be found in Washington, speaking his mind. But his perch is a bit loftier than it was on that August day when, as an impatient 23-year-old, he addressed the crowd immediately before Dr. King spoke. Today Lewis represents Georgia's 5th District in the U.S. House of Representatives.

In 1963 Lewis was the head of the Student Nonviolent Coordinating Committee (SNCC), one of the vanguard organizations fighting for civil rights. The son of sharecroppers, Lewis was a Freedom Rider in the early 1960s and was severely beaten by white mobs as he attempted to integrate long-segregated establishments in the South. As the head of SNCC, he was one of the six main organizers of the March on Washington, and he tangled with King and other top leaders when they saw the speech he had prepared. Among the phrases he agreed to drop just before he spoke were a threat to "burn Jim Crow to the ground" and a reference to the possibility that "we may be forced to march through the South the way Sherman did." But Lewis did say, "By the force of our demands, our determination and our numbers, we shall splinter the segregated South into a thousand pieces, and put them back together in the image of God and democracy." King's articulation of his dream proved a more unifying vision.

KING SPEAKS: A crowd of 200,000 people joined the Washington rally

What TIME Said Then

At the Memorial, the first order of business was a program of professional entertainment. Folk Singers Joan Baez, Josh White, Odetta, Bob Dylan, Peter-Paul-and-Mary rendered hymns and civil rights songs. Actor Marlon Brando brandished an electric cattle prod of the sort sometimes used by cops against civil rights demonstrators. Author James Baldwin, Actors Paul Newman, Burt Lancaster, Charlton Heston made appearances. —*Sept. 6, 1963*

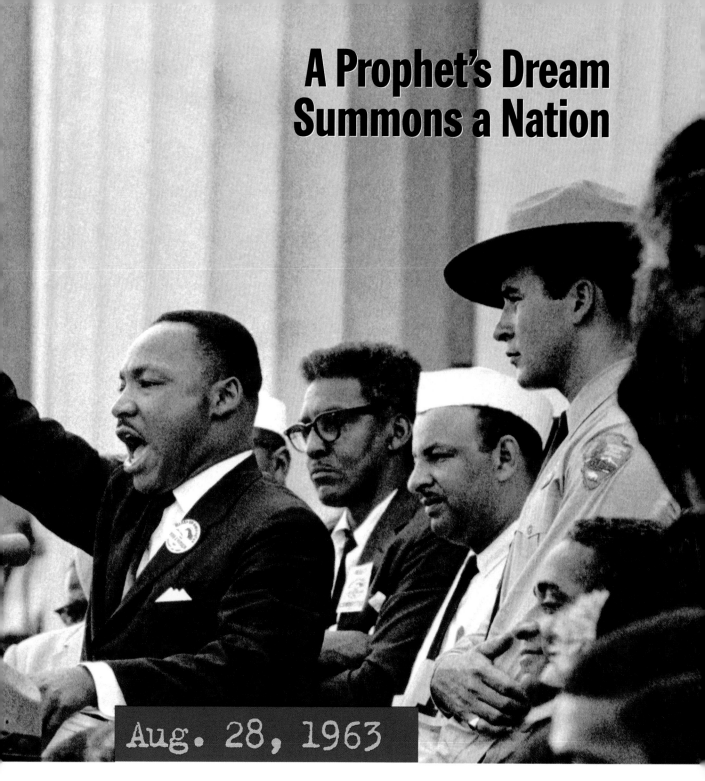

A Prophet's Dream Summons a Nation

Aug. 28, 1963

s a brilliant political speaker in his own right, John F. Kennedy observed Martin Luther King Jr.'s soul-stirring address to the huge throng at the Lincoln Memorial with a professional's eye. "He's damn good," he remarked to aides as they watched King on a TV set at the White House. According to King's biographer, Taylor Branch, Kennedy was especially impressed with King's departure from his prepared text to sound the electrifying refrain that became the oratorical high point of blacks' freedom struggle: "I have a dream that one day this nation will rise up and live out the true meaning of its creed ... I have

a dream that one day on the red hills of Georgia the sons of former slaves and the sons of former slave owners will be able to sit down together at a table of brotherhood ... I have a dream that my four children will one day live in a nation where they will not be judged by the color of their skin but by the content of their character."

A short time later, when King and other leaders of the March on Washington filed into the Cabinet Room to lobby for stronger provisions in Kennedy's proposed civil rights legislation, the President greeted King with a smile and a quip: "I have a dream."

—By Jack E. White

The Infamous Day in Dallas

Nov. 22, 1963

The backseat of President John F. Kennedy's limousine was a leather pit of horror, flecked with bits of flesh and a crust of drying blood that a grim young Secret Service agent was trying to wipe up with a sponge. He seemed hesitant, cowed by the task. On the front seat of the Lincoln lay the crushed red roses that Jackie Kennedy had been carrying. It was a certain and brutal end to a great national drama, but none of the people milling around on the driveway of Parkland Hospital that day wanted to allow the curtain to fall. Yet we knew it had.

I recall staring down into that miserable, tiny abattoir and shuddering and trying to understand that in a few seconds on a gloriously sunny day in an otherwise happy time, a friend had been murdered; a President assassinated; a political movement, which we called the New Frontier, terminated. We reporters had been riding casually in the press buses through a sunny, cheering downtown Dallas when we heard three sharp, strange sounds from an ugly building 50 yards in front of us. CBS correspondent Robert Pierpoint, who had covered the Korean War, leaped to his feet and

said, "Those sounded like gunshots." In a few seconds we saw the chaos on the grassy knoll, people facedown clutching the earth in panic, the motorcade chopped in two, Kennedy's limousine racing over a hill toward the hospital.

The monstrous event was confirmed at Parkland Hospital in small, prosaic episodes. Two priests arrived to give last rites, and coming out of the hospital, one of them blurted, "He's dead, all right." That was the first bulletin of death in a tragedy that was seizing the world, and for four more days would grow and be embedded in history by television saturation the likes of which we had never seen before.

Assistant press secretary Malcolm Kilduff took the podium in a stark hospital classroom and, reading off a scrap of paper that fluttered with his hand, announced, "President John F. Kennedy died at approximately 1 o'clock Central Standard Time today, here in Dallas." I remember wondering how anything as exuberant as the Kennedy Administration could end in such a simple sentence. Around the corner in his makeshift office, Kilduff sat mute, weeping. "Can you tell me anything more?" I asked as gently as I

LAST RITES The Kennedys arrive at Love Field; above, four key frames from Abraham Zapruder's film

■ Eyewitness to History

The man who took the most famous home movie in history was a Dallas garment manufacturer, Abraham Zapruder. His film was acquired for LIFE magazine by its Los Angeles bureau chief, Richard Stolley. Hearing the news of the assassination, Stolley

ZAPRUDER: He admired Kennedy

boarded a plane to Dallas; soon after his arrival he heard rumors about the film. Near midnight on Nov. 22, Stolley reached Zapruder at home and discovered to his surprise that no other reporter had contacted him. Stolley met Zapruder at his office the next morning and negotiated the rights for LIFE to acquire the film. Zapruder said he wanted LIFE to have the film because he trusted the magazine never to exploit his chance filming of the death of a man he deeply admired.

LIFE shared the film with government agencies; it was crucial evidence at the Warren Commission hearings. Zapruder died in 1970. Five years later, LIFE returned to his heirs the original film and all rights to its use—for which it had paid $150,000—for one dollar.

knew how. He tossed the announcement paper at me, then he whispered, "Oh, that man's head. Oh, his head."

Jackie Kennedy rested her hand on the casket as it was wheeled down the loading ramp of the hospital. For the first time we saw the bloodstains on her pink suit. She climbed into a white hearse with the lifeless body of her husband, while on the parking apron, the mortician argued with the Secret Service about payment for the casket and the car.

Lyndon Johnson took the presidential oath in the cramped fuselage of Air Force One, surrounded by Jackie, Lady Bird, aides from both staffs and a handful of reporters, leaning and pushing against one another to witness this historic moment. Soon afterward one of them, Sid Davis, the White House reporter for Westinghouse Broadcasting, climbed on the trunk of a car at the edge of Love Field and was relating the story of that frantic, improvised Inauguration. He had to pause as Air Force One roared down the runway and took off, heading back to Washington—the most devastating and yet the most historic flight that grand airplane had ever taken.   **—By Hugh Sidey**

What TIME Said Then

In a split second a thousand things happened. The President's body slumped to the left; his right leg shot up over the car door...there was a shocked, momentary stillness...then...a Secret Service man... flung himself across the trunk, and in his anger and frustration pounded it repeatedly with his fist. —*Nov. 29, 1963*

PROTEST DAYS: Dylan in 1963; Pete Seeger is at left

■ When Sullivan Balked, Dylan Walked

Many Americans recall the stunning shock of electricity that ran through the nation when the Beatles first played the *Ed Sullivan Show* early in 1964. But no one recalls Bob Dylan's scheduled appearance in May 1963— because it never took place. Dylan, then 21, had burst on America's folk scene much as the Beatles had on the British pop scene—with a freshness and raw talent that made everyone else seem instantly outdated. His repertoire included tongue-in-cheek updates of the old talking-blues format favored by his hero, Woody Guthrie. One of these was a song attacking a red-baiting cult group of the era, *Talkin' John Birch Society Paranoid Blues*. Sample lyrics: "So I run down most hurriedly/ And joined up with the John Birch Society,/ I got me a secret membership card/ And started off a-walkin' down the road. Yee-hoo, I'm a real John Bircher now!/ Look out you Commies!"

Clearly, this was not Topo Gigio. When a CBS network censor heard Dylan play the song in rehearsal on the day of the show, he declared it could not be sung on the air. Instead, he suggested Dylan sing a cover version of an innocuous song by the middle-of-the-road Irish folk group the Clancy Brothers. Dylan's response was recalled in 2002 by former teen star Brenda Lee, who had appeared on the program: "They said it was too political. He said, 'Then I won't do the show.' He picked up his guitar and harmonica, put his coat on and walked out the door. I stood there with my mouth open." Dylan was never again invited to appear on the show.

hey had first set foot in the U.S. only two days before. But their records— and their publicity—had preceded them: the Beatles, Britain's Fab Four, the sensation of Europe. Their single *I Want to Hold Your Hand* had just hit No. 1. That afternoon in Manhattan, hordes of fans—mostly adolescent, mostly female— surged in the street outside CBS's Studio 50, where the lads were rehearsing for their debut on the closest thing that era had to a national entertainment forum: Ed Sullivan's Sunday-night TV variety show. Later, a lucky few hundred of the faithful were seated in the theater. Well, sort of seated. They squirmed and thrashed, screamed and squealed, wept and shrieked.

To the reporters who were there, of whom I was one, covering the event for TIME, the noise was what seemed new. Surely these kids were louder, more frenzied, than Frank Sinatra's fans had ever been, or even Elvis Presley's. Sullivan made a pact with them before the show: Keep it down while other acts are on; otherwise you can do what you like.

So when the Beatles performed their five songs in two sets, the treble din engulfed the theater. You could hardly hear the music, but what did that matter? The Beatles' sheer presence was the point—their air of wholesome charm and cheeky wit, their instinctive connection with their audience. (It would be another couple of years before albums like *Revolver* and *Sgt. Pepper* showed that they were a musical phenomenon too.)

Sullivan, standing in front of his false curtain at stage right, peered out warily at the hysteria. You could almost see him thinking, What is this? What's going on? Many of us in the press were equally confounded, as probably were most of the estimated 73 million viewers who tuned in that night.

But Elvis knew. Earlier in the day in a telegram that couldn't help being symbolic he had wished the Beatles well. Elvis spoke as a product of the '50s. After the watershed Sullivan show, '60s pop culture, and all that it portended, both exhilarating and tragic, was in full cry. **—By Christopher Porterfield**

What TIME Said Then

The Beatles are being fueled by a genuine, if temporary, hysteria. In every part of the U.S. teen-agers are talking about little else, and superthatch Beatle-size wigs are being sold the hundreds of dozens. But part of the Beatles' peculiar charm is that they view it al with bemused detachment. — *Feb. 21, 1964*

1960s

Feb. 9, 1964

"Yeah, Yeah, Yeah!"

WATERSHED:
The Fab Four
with Sullivan at
a rehearsal for
the big show

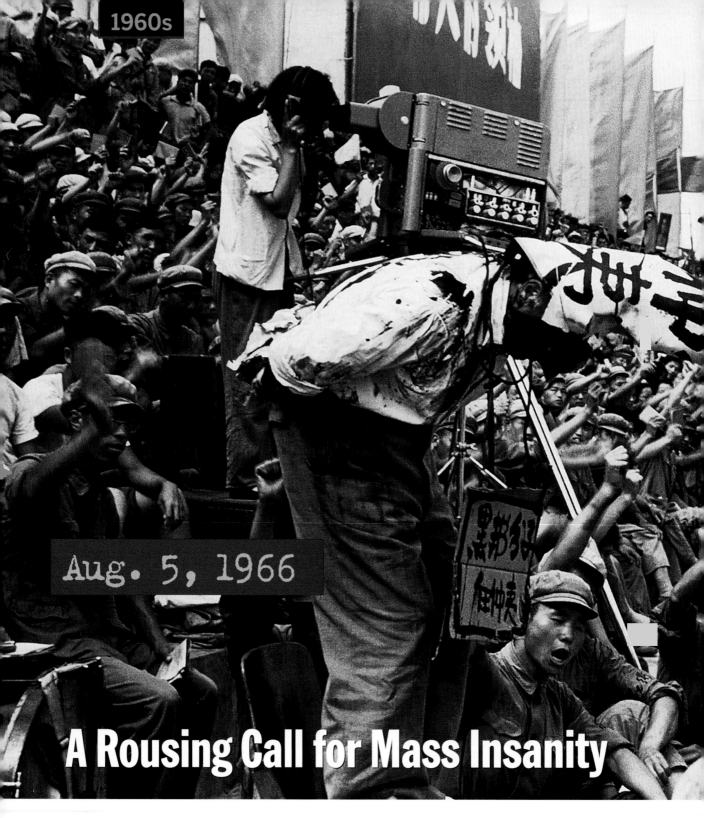

Aug. 5, 1966

A Rousing Call for Mass Insanity

The summer heat lay oppressively low on Shanghai, and Zheng Mingyi, 14, turned to the radio hoping for a diversion from the soaring mercury. What he heard that day changed his life and the lives of every citizen in the most populous nation on earth. In urgent tones, a news reader announced that Mao Zedong was exhorting citizens to rise up and "bombard the headquarters" to rid the party of his rivals and enemies. That day the Great Proletarian Cultural Revolution, announced two months before, took hold.

Schools were shuttered, and swarms of youths dubbed Red Guards began rampaging through the streets persecuting and sometimes killing anyone who was rich or educated or just plain outspoken. The madness lasted for a decade, during which millions were thrown into labor camps or forcibly relocated from cities to farms. The simplest things became crimes: wearing Western clothing, hoarding a slice of meat, forgetting a line from Mao's Little Red Book.

For Zheng, the crackly radio message that day meant the

ON TRIAL: Jiang Qing in court, 1976

LI ZHENSHENG, XINHUA NEWS AGENCY (INSET)

■ Midwife to Madness

Mao Zedong's wife Jiang Qing was one of the prime movers of China's disastrous Cultural Revolution. She was a popular Shanghai movie actress of 24 when she met Mao in 1937 as he and his Red Army were hiding out in remote Yunan province. Before long, Lan Ping, or Blue Apple, as she was then known, was pregnant by Mao, a married man 20 years her senior. Mao had to appeal to his Communist Party colleagues to obtain a divorce; they agreed, on the condition that Lan Ping never engage in political affairs.

Their follow-up was poor. Lan Ping became a strict party ideologue, changed her name to Jiang Qing (Azure River) and solidified her power base as leader of the nation's Marxist arts bureaucracy. She then used her muscle to avenge the party elders who had almost blocked her marriage to Mao—as well as the hapless actor who had refused to play Romeo opposite her Juliet back in her film days.

"Sex is engaging in the first rounds, but what sustains interest in the long run is power," Jiang told biographer Roxane Witke in 1972. Indeed, many scholars now see the Cultural Revolution as an interparty power struggle in which extreme leftists like Jiang used the Red Guards to dispatch their enemies. Jiang emerged triumphant from the period but lost her final struggle: she and three co-conspirators who hoped to seize power after Mao's death were arrested in 1976 and tried as the Gang of Four in a show trial.

After developing cancer in her later years, Jiang was released from prison and lived with her daughter under house arrest near Beijing. In June 1991, Chinese authorities confirmed the news—first revealed in TIME—that Jiang Qing had committed suicide the previous month by hanging herself.

dissolution of his family. He and his four siblings were dispersed across the country to remote villages as punishment for having a teacher as a father. By the time Zheng returned home seven years later, his father had been tortured by Red Guards and was dead. It was a tale repeated exponentially across the nation: Deng Xioaping, then a high party official, was purged twice, and his son was crippled for life. Even now when Zheng hears the radio start up, he shivers at what message the newscaster might bring.   **—By Hannah Beech**

Standing Up for Women's Rights

June 30, 1966

Sex discrimination" was added to Title VII of the 1964 Civil Rights Act. But there was no group to lobby for enforcement. I had written *The Feminine Mystique* in 1963, and I had become a magnet. Everyone was trying to pass the torch to me because I knew how to command media attention. Even a few surviving suffragists, who had chained themselves to the White House fence to win the vote, would call me up in the middle of the night and tell me to do something.

The government sought to pacify us and convened the Third National Conference of the Commissions on the Status of Women at the Washington Hilton in late June 1966. The omens were not good. That week President Johnson and Lady Bird invited a few of us to tea at the White House. The President said he wanted to appoint talented women, but the problem was "finding these women." It was a weekend of lip service.

We learned that we weren't allowed to pass resolutions at the conference. So on its final day, June 30, as dignitaries yammered away at the podium, I joined other furious women at the two front lunch tables, passing along notes written on napkins. We were putting together the National Organization for Women under the noses of the people who wanted to put us off. I wrote on one napkin that NOW had "to take the actions needed to bring women into the mainstream of American society, now … in fully equal partnership with men." As people rushed to catch planes, the founding members collected $5 from one another as our charter budget. Anna Roosevelt Halstead, Eleanor's daughter, gave me $10.   **—By Betty Friedan**

The Gift of a Brand-New Heart

I was 15 years old when Christiaan Barnard performed the first heart transplant. I still have the LIFE magazine cover. My dad was a cardiologist, so the drama carried out in the public's imagination was reinforced by my respect for the practice of medicine and discovery. My ultimate choice of going into surgery and then into heart surgery and then heart transplantation I trace back to that single operation.

This procedure reversed what had been inevitable death from heart disease, restoring the opportunity of new life. It demonstrated the ability of an individual working with a team to revolutionize health care. The interesting thing is that it was the relatively inexperienced Barnard who made history in the new field. He beat to the punch—and undercut—more systematic and more disciplined scientists and surgeons of the time. Dr. Norman Shumway of Stanford University (who was my mentor) had patiently and with great rigor made a decade of systematic research by writing papers, teaching others and working through the challenges of the procedure.

Barnard, who watched some of these procedures being carried out when he trained in the U.S., went back to South Africa and—with very little background and at the age of 45—seized the moment and performed this transplant. His patient died 18 days later, for Barnard was racing ahead of medicine's understanding of tissue rejection. But the pioneering spirit of that operation captured me at the time. **—By Bill Frist**

Frist is majority leader of the U.S. Senate.

What TIME Said Then

Barnard stepped back and ordered electrodes placed on each side of the heart and the current applied. The heart leaped at the shock and began a swift beat. Dr. Barnard's heart leaped too...through his mask he exclaimed, "Christ, it's going to work!" — *Dec. 15, 1967*

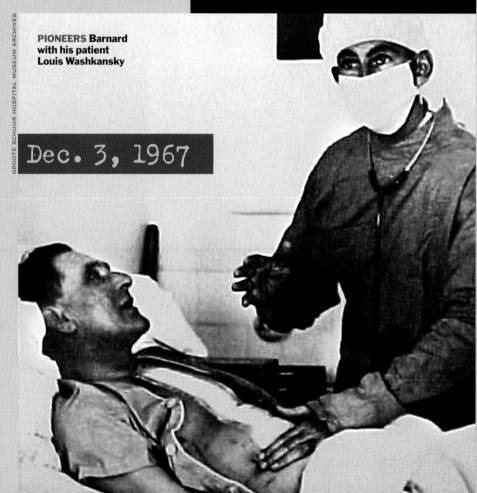

GROOTE SCHUUR HOSPITAL MUSEUM ARCHIVES

PIONEERS Barnard with his patient Louis Washkansky

Dec. 3, 1967

GIAP Tet's mastermind fought the Japanese, French and Americans

Jan. 31, 1968

BESIEGED: U.S. Marines take cover from sniper fire in Hué

BETTMANN CORBIS

■ The Red Napoleon

Admirers of Ho Chi Minh have dubbed him "the George Washington of Vietnam." But while Ho, like Washington, may have been "the indispensable man," General Vo Nguyen Giap was the military genius who won the pivotal victories of Vietnam's long war of indepedence. Giap organized the first "army" of the Viet Minh in 1944—34 men and 19 rifles—and took control of Hanoi a year later, after the Japanese pulled out. He was the mastermind behind the Viet Minh's victory over the French at Dienbienphu in 1954. He orchestrated the shocking success that was the Tet offensive and was in command of the army of North Vietnam when its tanks rolled into Saigon in 1975.

Giap called himself a "self-taught general." A former schoolteacher, he joined the Communist Party after reading Marx, and was arrested and jailed for three years in the 1930s as an agitator for Vietnamese independence from the French. His first wife and his sister-in-law died in French custody. Joining Ho to fight the French, he went to China to train with Mao Zedong's guerrillas, returning when World War II destabilized Indochina. Speaking to a U.S. reporter in 1990, Giap said, "We were not strong enough to drive out a half-million American troops, but that wasn't our aim. Our intention was to break the will of the American government to continue the war."

What TIME Said Then

Through the streets of Saigon, and in the dark approaches to dozens of towns and military installations across South Vietnam, other Vietnamese made their furtive way, intent on celebrating only death. After the last firecrackers had sputtered out on the ground, they struck with a fierceness and bloody destructiveness that Vietnam has not seen even in three decades of nearly continuous warfare. — *Feb. 9, 1968*

Tet: The Beginning of the End

P opular history tells us that American troops were caught napping when North Vietnam launched the Tet offensive. Yet while Vietnam celebrated its new year, at least one top U.S. Army officer was practically lying in wait. General Fred Weyand couldn't stop American officials in Saigon from throwing a party on Tet's eve, replete with Chinese firecrackers and a lawn band. Convinced of an imminent strike, however, Weyand kept his troops close to Saigon, and officers in his camp placed bets on the timing. All wagered that the strike would start between midnight and 5 a.m. on Jan. 31, and officers bet on

15-minute intervals, according to Neil Sheehan's *A Bright Shining Lie*. Saigon came under fire at about 3 a.m.

The U.S. and its South Vietnamese allies won the battle, but it proved an empty victory. The American public perceived the attack as a sign that the war was amounting to endless folly. The U.S. military's request for 206,000 more troops became politically unfeasible. Tet played a role in L.B.J.'s decision not to seek re-election. And young Army Major Colin Powell would later incorporate Tet's message into his doctrine that the U.S. should fight a war only with decisive force and vital interests at stake. —**By Daren Fonda**

April 4, 1968

OVER THERE!
King's aides point in the direction of the gunshot

In the Twilight, A Dreamer Dies

At 6:01 p.m., the Rev. Ralph David Abernathy stood before the mirror in room 306 of Memphis' Lorraine Motel, slapping on aftershave lotion in preparation for a soul-food dinner at the home of a local minister. His close friend Martin Luther King Jr. stood just outside the door on a second-floor concrete walkway, joshing with aides from the Southern Christian Leadership Conference who, like King, were in town to support striking sanitation workers.

Suddenly a sharp crack filled the air. Startled by what he thought was a firecracker, Abernathy looked out to the walk-

way and saw that King had fallen. Only his feet were visible, one foot protruding awkwardly through the walkway's iron railing. Abernathy rushed out, stepping over his friend to kneel by his side. Blood was gushing from a fist-size bullet wound in King's right cheek. Tenderly cradling King's head, Abernathy patted his left cheek and tried to console him: "This is Ralph, this is Ralph, Martin, don't be afraid." Moments later, another King aide, Andrew Young, checked King's pulse and told Abernathy, "Ralph, it's all over." Still rocking King in his arms, Abernathy sobbed, "Don't say that, don't say that." The grief others felt for the martyred civil rights leader would set off days of rioting across America.
— *By Jack E. White*

What TIME Said Then

In Memphis, through the budding branches of trees surrounding a tawdry rooming house, a white sniper's bullet cut down Dr. Martin Luther King Jr., pre-eminent voice for the just aspirations and long-suffering patience of black America. —*April 12, 1963*

Camelot's Last Shining Moment

H e was a latecomer to the race, and Democratic elders, already reeling from President Lyndon Johnson's waning popularity and from Eugene McCarthy's antiwar campaign, had urged the New York senator not to run. But Robert F. Kennedy proved a formidable sprinter. For 80 days he campaigned relentlessly, and by the day of the California primary, a must-win for Kennedy to seriously challenge Hubert Humphrey, his body was cracking. The night before, he had been too weary to finish a speech in San Diego, and by the time he reached Los Angeles, he appeared to be running on fumes.

On primary night, however, the old Kennedy vigor returned. His suite at the Ambassador Hotel filled with well-wishers, and as the results turned his way, campaign workers began "laughing and dancing and hugging one another," recalled his aide, former pro-football player Roosevelt Grier. Around midnight Kennedy went downstairs and delivered a rousing speech to 1,800 supporters in the ballroom. He then exited through the hotel's pantry, where at 12:16 a.m., a slight, dark-haired Palestinian named Sirhan Sirhan pulled out a .22-cal. revolver, fired eight shots and fatally wounded the candidate. For a stricken America, the assassination revived memories of the killings of Kennedy's brother John and of Martin Luther King Jr. and shattered the dreams of those yearning for a return to Camelot.

—By Daren Fonda

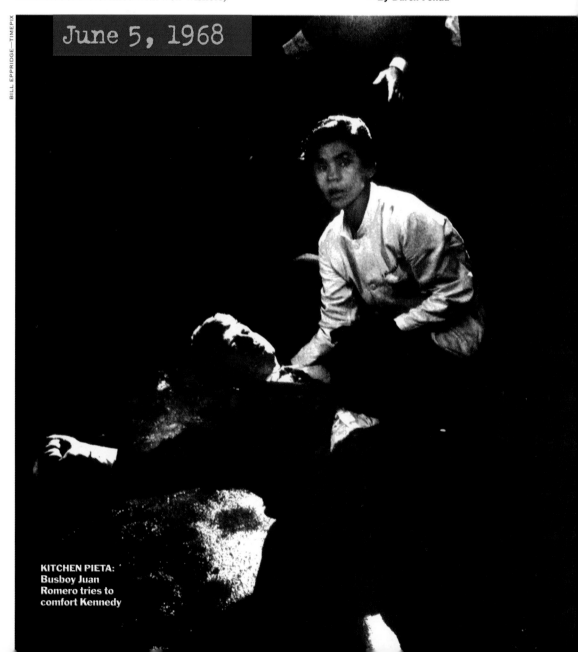

June 5, 1968

BILL EPPRIDGE—TIMEPIX

KITCHEN PIETA:
Busboy Juan
Romero tries to
comfort Kennedy

Gays Find Their Voices

It was 1:20 a.m. when eight cops stomped into the Stonewall Inn, a dive in Manhattan's Greenwich Village district that had no liquor license but served watery drinks to a mix of drag queens, street kids, gay professionals and closeted and straight mafiosi (who ran the place). Within two hours, the Village was bleeding and burning as hundreds rioted.

How did the nightly saturnalia at Stonewall produce protests that would kick start the modern gay-rights movement? The uprising was inspirited by a potent cocktail of pent-up rage (raids of gay bars were brutal and routine), overwrought emotions (hours earlier, thousands had wept at the funeral of Judy Garland) and drugs. As a 17-year-old cross-dresser was being led into the paddy wagon and got a shove from a cop, she fought back. "[She] hit the cop and was so stoned, she didn't know what she was doing—or didn't care," one of her friends later told Martin Duberman, author of the history *Stonewall*.

Later, the deputy police inspector in charge would explain that day's impact: "For those of us in [the] public morals [division], things were completely changed ... Suddenly they were not submissive anymore." Today gays and lesbians recall that night each year with a weekend of rallies, parades and parties—a spectacle as inspiring and raunchy as the Stonewall itself. **—By John Cloud**

June 28, 1969

LIBERATED: Revelers celebrate their new movement outside New York City's Stonewall Inn

FRED MCDARRAH

What TIME Said Then

On the moon even the taciturn Armstrong could not contain his excitement...he began to...snap pictures with all the enthusiasm of the archetypal tourist. Houston had to remind him four times to quit clicking...— *July 25, 1969*

In One Man's Footstep, A Giant Stride Forward

Neil Armstrong meant to say "That's one small step for a man," adapting a phrase from a children's playground game. Instead, because of intense radio static, Mission Control in Houston—and the rest of mankind—heard, "That's one small step for ... man, one giant leap for mankind," which became one of the most famous sentences of the 20th century. If the audio failed, the images were indelible, as a camera mounted on the base of

July 20, 1969

the lunar-landing vehicle beamed back the otherworldly milestone. Ohio-born Armstrong, then 38, had become the first earthling on the moon. He was almost immediately followed by Colonel Edwin (Buzz) Aldrin, who helped plant a U.S. flag, signifying to all the world that America had won the race that had begun 12 years earlier with the launch of the Soviet Union's Sputnik. The stakes? Armstrong says that he "was certainly aware that this was the culmination of the work of 300,000 or 400,000 people over a decade."

There were three reasons that Armstrong—a naval aviator in the Korean War who had flown 78 combat missions—became the first to step on the moon. He had returned to civilian life, and the Nixon Administration, mired in the Vietnam War, did not want a commissioned officer "militarizing" space. Second, his reticent manner was considered ideal for coping with the demands of celebrityhood. Third, and most practical, as mission commander he was physically closer to the hatch of the *Eagle* and had to be the first out. Since Armstrong was assigned to handle the camera, most of the pictures from that famous mission are of Aldrin, with Armstrong seen only as a reflection on the colonel's helmet. With Michael Collins, who piloted the command module above them, the astronauts became latter-day Lindberghs, receiving parades and honors in 22 countries. Twelve other men would walk on the moon, the last in 1972.

—By Douglas Brinkley

NIKITA KHRUSHCHEV AND JOHN F. KENNEDY
At their Vienna summit, June 3, 1961, the Soviet boss shook J.F.K. with his disdain for the deaths that might arise from nuclear war. Fresh from the Bay of Pigs debacle, J.F.K. predicted: "It's going to be a cold winter." The frost came earlier: the Soviets built the Berlin Wall in August

FRED SCHUTZER—TIMEPIX

ZOE DOMINIC—PIX INC.—TIMEPIX

Fateful Meetings

MARGOT FONTEYN AND RUDOLPH NUREYEV
The 23-year-old Russian stepped out of a London taxi on Nov. 11, 1961, to meet Fonteyn, at 42 the world's leading ballerina. She had invited the recent defector to join her in a benefit. They clicked, and a legendary series of pas de deux began

RICHARD BURTON AND ELIZABETH TAYLOR
The first scene *Cleopatra*'s two leads shot together called for a passionate embrace. On the morning of Jan. 22, 1962, they got the scene perfect on the first take, but when the director yelled "Cut!"—they lingered in each other's arms. Within weeks, both abandoned their marriages

EVERETT COLLECTION

Snapshots

■ Joan Baez

Her voice is as clear as air in the autumn, a vibrant, untrained, thrilling soprano. She wears no makeup, and her long black hair hangs like a drapery, parted around her long almond face. She walks straight to the microphone and begins to sing. No patter. No show business. She wears a sweater and skirt, or something semi-Oriental that seems to have been hand-sewn out of burlap. **—Nov. 23, 1962**

■ Julia Child

When a potato pancake falls on the worktable, she scoops it back into the pan, bats her big blue eyes at the cameras, and advises: "Remember, you're all alone in the kitchen and no one can see you." **—Nov. 25, 1966**

■ Cassius Clay

There were times when people wondered if he was real. Crowds stopped to gawk at the tall, brown gladiator as he ambled along the Via Veneto, grinning, waving, talking to everybody whether they understood him or not. He captured Bing Crosby and went everywhere with him arm in arm. He brushed off a Russian reporter who prodded him about the plight of U.S Negroes: "Man, the U.S.A. is the best country in the world, counting yours. I ain't fighting off alligators and living in a mud hut."

In the Olympic Village, he swarmed over foreign athletes, yelling "Say cheese!" while he snapped photos, swapped team badges, slapped backs, and winked at pretty girls. They loved him. **—March 22, 1963**

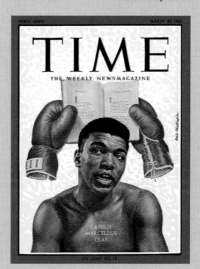

■ Hugh Hefner

Bacchanalia with Pepsi. Orgies with popcorn. And 24 girls—count 'em, 24—living right overhead! It is all so familiar and domestic. Don Juan? Casanova? That was in another country and, besides, the guys are dead. Hugh Hefner is alive, American, modern, trustworthy, clean, respectful, and the country's leading impresario of spectator sex. He realized the old taboos were going, and he took the old-fashioned, shame-thumbed girlie magazine, stripped off the plain wrapper, added gloss, class and culture. It was a surefire formula. **—March 3, 1967**

■ Vince Lombardi

Lombardi studied so many movies of old Green Bay games that his eyes were constantly bloodshot. He yelled so loud at practice that he lost his voice. In pre-game pep talks, Lombardi's speeches were like something out of the *The Spirit of Notre Dame*. Once he got down on his knees in the locker room and led the team in the Lord's Prayer. "You wouldn't think a pro coach could get away with that stuff," says a player. "But he did."

"I'll never forget the speech he made before the first league game in 1959, his first year," says Linebacker Bill Forester. "He ended it by yelling 'Go through that door and bring back a victory!' I jumped up and hit my arm on my locker. It was my worst injury of the year." **—May 7, 1968**

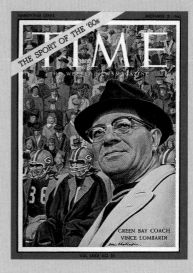

1970s

JULY 4, 1976 Americans did their best to celebrate the nation's Bicentennial, but with an unelected President in the Oval Office and Saigon's fall still fresh in memory, the festivities were muted

OCT. 11, 1975 When *Saturday Night Live* debuted on NBC, it was TV's first showcase for the era's radical humor. From left, original cast members Chevy Chase, John Belushi, Garrett Morris, Laraine Newman, Gilda Radner, Jane Curtin and Dan Ackroyd

Still reeling from the over-the-top '60s, America never caught its breath in the '70s. A President fell over a second-rate burglary, Saigon fell to the communists, and we all fell for disco. Sometimes it seemed as if the only thing rising in the '70s was the price of gas

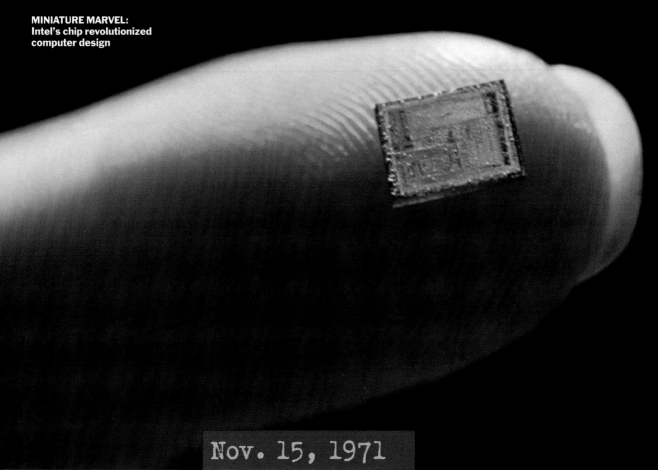

Nov. 15, 1971

When the Big Idea Was a Little Chip

Back when I was in charge of Intel's manufacturing and engineering, we were in the throes of introducing a new product: a set of microchips, which we used in combinations to build everything from calculators to postage meters. They were electronic Lego blocks of sorts. Beyond that, they were chips like any others we were building in those days and if anything simpler than the complex memory chips that occupied our attention. So it was with amazement that we manufacturing types greeted the trade-paper ad that appeared on Nov. 15: "Announcing a New Era of Integrated Electronics," it trumpeted. Frankly, I was horrified; what was this new era? What was so special? Looking back, the marketing folks were on to something. Digital electronics was growing rapidly. Customers began demanding improvements leading to more and more complex versions of the building blocks. We called them microprocessors, and they became the soul of the personal computer.   **—By Andrew Grove**

Grove is the chairman of the board of Intel.

TOP TRIO Grove, left, with Intel's Robert Noyce and Gordon Moore in 1975

A Botched Burglary Fells a President

The gambit was actually the burglars' second break-in at the Democratic National Committee's headquarters in the Watergate office-apartment-hotel complex. The first time they bugged the phone, but on this night they were trying to fix the inoperative listening device. Sent by President Nixon's re-election committee, they set off a cascade of stupidity by taping open the lock on an office door, wrapping the tape in such a way as to be visible to building guard Frank Wills. The first time he saw the gray tape, he peeled it off and threw it away. When he noticed that someone had replaced it, he called the cops.

The political espionage was utterly unnecessary. Richard Nixon was going to win in a landslide anyway. Rather than fire all those responsible for the break-in, Nixon instead paid the five arrested burglars hush money from an illegal White House slush fund; urged the CIA to close down the FBI investigation; told his subordinates to lie to investigators; discussed a variety of illegal cover-up plans in the Oval Office, knowing a tape recorder was already in operation there; fired the special prosecutor for the case who had been hired by his Justice Department; defied court orders to turn over the tapes; and then, faced with certain impeachment by Congress, announced his resignation on Aug. 8, 1974, the only American President ever to quit the job. The scandal poisoned national politics and undermined public trust in government for decades.

—By John F. Stacks

SCENE OF THE CRIME
The second burglary was bungled, but it was the cover-up that brought down Nixon

June 17, 1972

Jan. 22, 1973

Women Get the Right to Choose

The world was about to change for women that Monday morning, but only the nine U.S. Supreme Court Justices and a few court personnel knew it. The second case on the docket that day was *Roe v. Wade*, which challenged the Texas laws making virtually all abortions illegal. Justice Harry Blackmun read the decision, for which he had written the majority opinion, declaring the laws unconstitutional. The vote was 7 to 2.

I was in Austin, Texas, a recently elected legislator, and unaware of what was going on in Washington, even though I had filed and argued *Roe v. Wade*. *Roe* began in 1969 when a group of University of Texas graduate students asked whether they could be prosecuted as accomplices to abortion if they shared information about where to get illegal abortions or out-of-state legal ones. I was 24, a woman lawyer and willing to do the case for free. We found a 1965 Supreme Court case overturning a Connecticut law making it a crime to use birth control, as well as cases in other states challenging antiabortion statutes. We decided to challenge the Texas laws. A pregnant woman called Jane Roe was the plaintiff in the class action suit we

filed against Henry Wade, the district attorney of Dallas County.

As Blackmun's words faded in D.C. that Monday, phones began ringing in the law offices my husband Ron and I shared. We learned from reporters that we had won. But we didn't know exactly what the court's decision said until a friend in Washington got a copy and read the entire document to me over the phone. It said women had a constitutional right to make private decisions about whether to continue or terminate a pregnancy, and that the state had not proven a compelling reason to regulate that. Abortion was legal.

A woman scheduled to leave Austin on a 3 p.m. flight for a California abortion was instead given one by her local doctor that afternoon. After *Roe*, the ability of women to make choices expanded. But the controversy did not end. Thirty years later, the debate over abortion law has only intensified.

—By Sarah Weddington

Weddington is founder of the Weddington Center, which promotes leadership skills.

STEPPING UP "Jane Roe" (Norma McCorvey) visits the Supreme Court in 1989

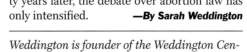

UPPER HUDSON PLANNED PARENTHOOD®

After 16 Years: Good Night, Vietnam

PLAN TO CLOSE MISSION AT ABOUT 0430 30 APRIL LOCAL TIME. DUE TO NECESSITY TO DESTROY [COMMUNICATIONS] GEAR THIS IS THE LAST MESSAGE FROM EMBASSY SAIGON.

Once the words above were sent to America, someone took a sledge-hammer to the machinery. The ambassador and CIA chief were flown out by 5 a.m., and the last official American presence—11 Marines—waited for a helicopter on the roof. Around them, chaos had blossomed: Saigon was burning, the communists were nearing, and thousands of South Vietnamese were trying to flee with the Americans. Hours earlier, one man had tried to put his baby on an embassy bus, as ABC's Ken Kashiwahara re-

TRIUMPH Soldiers of North Vietnam's army troop into Saigon

calls in the oral history *Tears Before the Rain*. Kashiwahara watched as the man fell, and the bus ran over the baby. But the driver kept going.

Just before 8 a.m., a Chinook-46 helicopter landed and whisked away those last Marines, drawing up plumes of the tear gas they had dispersed in the embassy to discourage people from going to the roof. And in that vaporous haze, the American war in Vietnam—a debacle that took 16 years and 58,000 American lives—finally ended.

—*By John Cloud*

April 30, 1975

April 1, 1976

THE SEED **Wozniak, left, Jobs and the guts of the Apple 1**

Apple Boots Up

They were two guys named Steve, so Steve Jobs was called Steve and Steve Wozniak went by Woz. At 25, Wozniak was the technical brains. Jobs, 21, was the dreamer with a knack for getting others to dream along with him. They had attended the same high school, and in the hazy years after graduation—both were college dropouts—a shared interest in electronics brought them together. Jobs didn't yet have his own place, so when their formal business partnership began, the decision to work together was made in a bedroom at his parents' ranch house in Los Altos, Calif.

Most computers in 1976 were room-size machines with Defense Department–size price tags, but Wozniak had been tinkering with a new design, and his computer was different. It wasn't much to look at— just a bunch of chips screwed to a piece of plywood— but it was small, cheap and easy to use, and Jobs had noticed the stir it caused when they took it to a local computer club. "He said, 'We'll make it for 20 bucks, sell it for 40 bucks!'" Wozniak remembers. "I kind of didn't think we'd do it." Jobs came up with the name, inspired by an orchard in Oregon where he had worked with some friends: Apple Computer. "When we started the little partnership, it was just like, Oh, this will be fun," Wozniak says. "We won't make any money, but it'll be fun."

They didn't go out and celebrate that day. Woz wouldn't even quit his day job designing chips for calculators at Hewlett-Packard until months later, after Jobs had sold his Volkswagen bus for seed money. Nobody, not even Jobs, saw what was coming next: that Apple would create the look and feel of every desktop in the world and start our love affair with the personal computer. —*By Lev Grossman*

The Arrival of the Jedi

The film wasn't supposed to do what it did—nothing was supposed to do that. Movies were meant to stay on the screen, flat and large and colorful, gathering you up into their sweep of story and releasing you back into your life at the other end. But this movie misbehaved. *Star Wars* leaked out of the theater, poured off the screen. A lot of people were affected deeply by it, requiring talismans and artifacts, merchandising and sequels.

The day of the premiere bewildered me. The movie was attracting giddy attention that was both exciting and unsettling. So there we were—Harrison Ford, Mark Hamill and I— jittery and on live talk shows (like acid, only more gruesomely populated), and throughout the day we attempted to deliver George Lucas' message to enlist in his "star war." Harrison was its most apparently able representative; Mark and I were clambering to get up to speed. After all, we were fig-

uring out who we were, forming our public, never-before-aired personas in front of you, perfecting our act by the seat of our talk-show pants. But we all liked the attention. What immature actor doesn't? Of course Harrison might have been mature, but I barely noticed, being self-obsessed and 20; he, 34, was an icon right out of the solar chute. We giggled and ran from chasing fans and were amazed. Suddenly we went from being a carpenter, a TV actor and a movie star's kid to looking like three of the new "Fab Four" (George Lucas being John, and you can mix and match the rest.)

The recorded opening date was May 25, but the thundering hooves of asteroid arrival and Death Star intervention had started many days before. It wasn't like a movie opening; it was like an earthquake. Each day that got closer to the film's release, a signal went out: a high-pitched dog whistle, not audible to the human ear but heard by sci-fi geeks everywhere, generating an excitement in the atmosphere like electricity. It crackled around the theaters. It hummed above my head. I don't know how it started; all I know is that suddenly it was everywhere. It was picked up first by the new order of geeks, enthusiastic young people with sleeping bags. "It" was coming, and they wanted to experience it first: to sit in the dark, the shadow and light of space battle flashing on their spellbound faces. And they came back over and over again. I drove by at least one long, snaking line in Westwood, holding down the humiliating urge to screech, "Yes! I am Princess Leia Organa, come to tell you all, come to tell you all!" But what had I come to tell them? So I didn't say anything. I just stared in amazement and wondered what it would ultimately mean. And now, when an old man of 43 or so strolls timidly up to me and exclaims how as a young boy he loved me, I almost know. **—By Carrie Fisher**

Fisher (Princess Leia) is now an author and screenwriter.

May 25, 1977

FORCE FRENZY
The movie was a sensation at Mann's Theater in L.A. Inset: Mark Hamill, Carrie Fisher and Harrison Ford in their famemaking roles

Evening News

LATE SPECIAL CITY PRICES

BRITAIN'S BIGGEST EVENING SALE

LONDON: THURSDAY JULY 27 1978

Meet Louise, the world's first test-tube arrival

SUPERBABE

Wide-eyed Louise Brown pictured in hospital 18 hours after she was born. Today she's doing well. See Page Three

ASSOCIATED NEWSPAPERS

July 25, 1978

Brave New Baby

Even before Louise Brown arrived, the London tabloids called her "Our Miracle Baby," and critics muttered words like Frankenstein. The world's first test-tube baby, she was born at 13 minutes to midnight—a 5-lb. 12-oz. bundle of squealing ethical questions and implications for the future of the species. After hundreds of tries, Lesley Brown's doctors found the secret to creating a baby outside the womb: having fertilized her egg in vitro, or in a Petri dish, they implanted the embryo after only 2½ days rather than waiting for five and were rewarded with their first successful pregnancy. But the breakthrough was not chronicled in some journal of reproductive medicine. The whole world awaited the birth because at the suggestion of one of their doctors, the parents had negotiated exclusive rights to the first baby pictures with the London *Daily Mail* for more than $500,000. Newspapers that bought reprint rights were guaranteed a 40% discount if the baby died within the first week.

It was the rare commentator who avoided any mention of Aldous Huxley. Some warned of baby farms and assembly lines of fetuses grown in test tubes, of rich women renting poor women's wombs to avoid the inconvenience of pregnancy. But fear was no match for dreams for thousands of infertile couples: "I would hope that within a very few years ... this will be a fairly commonplace affair," said Robert Edwards, one of the doctors. Louise is now 24, and 1 million babies later, that prophecy has come true.   **—By Nancy Gibbs**

An Exiled Prophet Returns to Iran

From the perspective of nearly 2½ decades, the success of the Islamic revolution in Iran and its monumental impact across the Islamic world may appear to have been inevitable. It seemed like anything but certain destiny, however, to those of us on board the Air France 747 taking Ayatullah Ruhollah Khomeini from Paris to Tehran that morning in 1979.

The exiled Shah's Prime Minister, Shahpour Bakhtiar, still controlled the country and commanded the armed forces, and our immediate concern was whether the air force might decide that the best way to solve the problem of the radical fundamentalist leader would be to blow us out of the sky. That threat didn't intimidate the Ayatullah, who calmly went to sleep on the cabin floor, resting up for his arrival in Tehran, where he would be greeted by more than 1 million cheering supporters.

It would take eight tumultuous days before Khomeini could wrest power from Bakhtiar, but already in his arrival speech he abandoned earlier hints of willingness to share power and demanded that the Prime Minister get out. Tipped off that the military was going to arrest him, Khomeini broadcast an appeal that brought tens of thousands of Iranians into the streets. Stores of weapons in the mosques were flowing into the hands of Khomeini loyalists, and a bloody civil war appeared almost certain.

Shortly before dawn on Feb. 9, amid some fighting in downtown Tehran, I was hunkered in a bank entrance. Virtually everyone carried a weapon, even children. Armed revolutionaries manned checkpoints at every corner. A boy of about 11 pointed an automatic rifle at my chest, safety off, and asked for identification, which he couldn't read. After considerable vacillation, the military leadership declared its neutrality. The Ayatullah went on radio to announce, "The dictatorship has abandoned its last trench."

That November, radical supporters seized the American embassy, provoking a 444-day confrontation with the "Great Satan" over 52 hostages. But Khomeini never was able to reconcile the widely divergent forces in his revolution. Top aides fled into exile or were executed, and thousands of other were imprisoned or killed. Iran became deeply divided and remains so today. Despite this, to Khomeini's neighbors in the Arab world the Ayatullah's revolution serves as a historical beacon. —*By Bruce van Voorst*

Van Voorst was TIME's *Middle East bureau chief in 1979-80.*

Feb. 1, 1979

HE'S BACK
Khomeini greets supporters shortly after his return

A Soviet Power Play in Afghanistan

The Afghan department in the Soviet foreign ministry was one of the quietest spots in the U.S.S.R.'s diplomatic service. But when Afghanistan's nonalignment policy began to slip, the Soviet leadership panicked. Three members of the Kremlin's inner circle—Foreign Minister Andrei Gromyko, KGB chief Yuri Andropov and Defense Minister Dmitri Ustinov—feared that the Afghans would tilt toward the U.S. unless stern "measures" were taken. Late on the night of Dec. 12, ailing Communist Party chairman Leonid Brezhnev called the three to a secret meeting to hear their pro-

posal. To keep the U.S. from installing a friendly regime, they said, Moscow must send in troops. The military operation, Brezhnev was told, would be over in three or four weeks.

Two weeks later, the Soviets began an invasion that was to last nearly a decade and chill U.S.-Soviet relations for years. By the law of unintended consequences, the U.S. decision to back an anti-Soviet guerrilla force, the *mujahedin*, was to rebound disastrously with the rise of Islamic terrorism, when Osama bin Laden eventually found in the shattered Afghanistan a vital haven. **—By Johanna McGeary**

Dec. 12, 1979

PETER MARLOW—MAGNUM

VICTORY! First to shatter Britain's gender barrier, Thatcher would remain P.M. until late 1990

May 3, 1979

...was the most brutal ...ow from the Soviet ...nion's steel fist since the ...d Army's invasion of ...echoslovakia in 1968. ... a lightning series of ...ents last week, Afghan-...an's President Hafizul-...h Amin was overthrown, ...d subsequently exe-...ted, in a ruthless coup ...ounted by the Soviet ...nion. —*Jan. 7, 1980*

MOVING IN: Soviet troops take command of the airport in Kabul

The Iron Lady Spreads Her Wings

Margaret Thatcher arrived at her North London constituency early, in good time for glad-handing and a last bit of publicity. But it was well into the following morning when the last paper ballots from every village and shire came in: the gutsy politician of the zealous right had routed Labour Prime Minister James Callaghan to become Britain's first female PM.

On the doorstep of her new residence, 10 Downing Street, the new leader cited the compassionate litany of St. Francis of Assisi: "Where there is discord, let there be harmo-

ny." It would be the last conciliatory message from this aggressive, even strident, Prime Minister, who boasted, "I am not a consensus politician, I am a conviction politician!" Her conservative creed transformed Britain: she broke the unions' stranglehold, flogged the business world out of complacency, altered the welfare-state mentality and boldly fought a war over the Falkland Islands, some 8,000 miles away. And she did it all her way.

—By Bonnie Angelo

Angelo, TIME's *London bureau chief from 1978 to 1985, published* First Mothers *in 2000.*

BLACK STAR

JOHN SHEARER — TIMEPIX

MAO ZEDONG AND RICHARD NIXON
The ailing 78-year-old Chairman, meeting Nixon at his Beijing home, noted apologetically, "I can't talk very well." But talk they did, for nearly an hour— after almost 25 years of silence between their nations. A great wall had fallen

TRAINING HDQTS.
JOE FRAZIER
HEAVYWEIGHT
CHAMPION

Fateful Meetings

DAVID HUME KENNERLY — GETTY IMAGES FOR TIME

ANWAR SADAT AND MENACHEM BEGIN
Unlike Moses' journey, Sadat's across the Sinai was not a lengthy trip— his plane touched down a minute early on Nov. 19, 1977— but the Egyptian leader had to traverse the obstacle of mutual distrust to clasp the hand of his erstwhile enemy in Jerusalem

MUHAMMAD ALI AND JOE FRAZIER For Ali, their 1971 fight—his comeback after a jail term for draft refusal—was about race and redemption. For Frazier, it was about shutting Ali up. (Ali had mocked him as an Uncle Tom and a "gorilla.") Frazier won the March 8 match by a decision in 15 rounds, setting the stage for two historic rematches

Snapshots

Sam Ervin

The jowls jiggled. The eybrows rolled in waves. The words tumbled out disarmingly, but they conveyed his moral outrage. "Divine right went out with the American Revolution and doesn't belong to White House aides," Sam Ervin said. "What meat do they eat that makes them grow so great? That is not Executive privilege. It is Executive poppycock." **—April 16, 1973**

Patty Hearst

In the bewilderment shared by all who have followed the case, her anguished father Randolph A. Hearst exclaimed: "It's terrible! Sixty days ago, she was a lovely child. Now there's a picture of her in a bank with a gun in her hand." **—April 29, 1974**

Joe Namath

In his youth he ignored his studies for the pursuit of pigskin and other cutaneous diversions. In setting a career for himself as a professional, Joe snubbed the St. Louis Cardinals of the older National Football League in favor of the New York Jets of the lowly American Football League.

Even then he did not play by the rules. His clothes were too loud. His lip was too loose. There were wild tales of girls and booze, of riotous pre-dawn odysseys through Manhattan saloons. What good could come of such a rogue?

What good indeed? At 29, after six, turbulent, injurious seasons, Joe Namath has established himself as the pre-eminent quarterback in professional football today. **—Oct. 16, 1972**

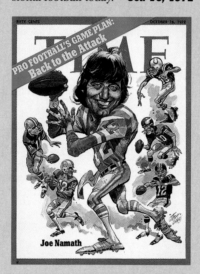

Alexander Solzhenitsyn

Solzhenitsyn was first stripped and searched, then dressed in prison garb. He was questioned for several hours by a team of interrogators, and was told that the charge against him was treason, for which the maximum punishment is death. Just as another great Russian writer, Fyodor Dostoyevsky, was placed before a sham firing squad 125 years ago, so was Solzhenitsyn subjected to a similarly cruel mockery. Although the Soviets planned all along to deport him to the West, he was locked in a cell that night under the threat of the death penalty. **—Feb. 25, 1974**

Mother Teresa

Mother Teresa remembers finding a dying woman on a Calcutta sidewalk, her feet half chewed away by rats, her wounds alive with maggots. Only with great difficulty did she persuade a hospital to take the woman. Within days the nun was pleading with authorities for "just one room" to which she could take the dying. What they gave her was a onetime pilgrims' rest house near the Temple of Kali, the Hindu goddess of death. She renamed it Nirmal Hriday (Pure Heart) and filled it.

Nirmal Hriday is now only one of 32 havens for the dying, 67 leprosariums, 28 children's homes that Mother Teresa's order runs round the world, but it still moves visitors to wonderment. **—Dec. 29, 1975**

It was the age of Reagan: Go for it! Americans walked tall, yuppies ate sushi and Wall Street's "Masters of the Universe" bayed for cash. The era began with U.S. hostages languishing in Tehran and ended with the fall of the Berlin Wall. 'Nuf said?

1980s

JULY 13, 1985 The Live Aid concert, televised globally from London and Philadelphia, caught the idealistic, if naive, impulses of the age: rockers in the First World united in song to help the victims of famine in Africa. Center, concert organizer Bob Geldof

FEB. 22, 1980 The U.S. hockey team beat the U.S.S.R. in the Olympic Games at Lake Placid, N.Y., 13 days after losing to the Soviets, 10-3, in an exhibition match

JULY 4, 1986 Coming at a high-water mark of U.S. prestige and power, the dedication of the lovingly restored Statue of Liberty seemed the bicentennial celebration the U.S. denied itself in 1976

SEC. 135. CERTAIN CASH OR DEFERRED ARRANGEMENTS.

(a) IN GENERAL.—Section 401 (relating to qualified pension, profit-sharing, and stock bonus plans) is amended by redesignating subsection (k) as (l) and by inserting after subsection (j) the following new subsection:

"(k) CASH OR DEFERRED ARRANGEMENTS.—

"(1) GENERAL RULE.—A profit-sharing or stock bonus plan shall not be considered as not satisfying the requirements of subsection (a) merely because the plan includes a qualified cash or

A Good Day for Savers

On a quiet Saturday afternoon, I came in to work at my benefits-consulting firm without the distraction of a ringing telephone and co-workers wandering into my office. I was there redesigning the retirement program for one of our bank clients. As I was considering the bank's goals, I was drawn to Section 401(k) of the Internal Revenue Code. Seeking a tax break and an edge over its competitors, the bank wanted to replace its cash-bonus plan with a deferred-profit-sharing plan under which employees wouldn't have access to the money until they left the bank. I realized that Section 401(k), which had become effective on Jan. 1, would allow me to do that. I could use this section to design a plan allowing each employee to put in whatever portion of the cash bonus he or she wanted. People who put money into the plan would get a tax break, but I knew it wouldn't be attractive enough to get many of the lower-paid employees to participate. A bit of desperation got the creative juices flowing. That was when I thought of offering a matching employer contribution as an additional incentive.

At this point the potential of what I had just "created" hit. Most large employers at the time had savings plans in which employees put in money after taxes and received a matching employer contribution. I immediately realized it would be possible to change those plans so that employees would be able to put their money in before taxes rather than after. The bank client rejected the idea because its attorney didn't want the bank to do something that had never been done. As a result, the first plan we did was for our own employees. And this is what started the 401(k) savings-plan revolution. **—By Ted Benna**

Benna is a retirement-planning consultant to businesses.

Identifying a Modern Plague

Almost everybody who had an interest in the situation was represented there that pleasant summer Tuesday in Washington, including gay-community leaders, federal bureaucrats and the investigative team from the Centers for Disease Control and Prevention (CDC) that had taken a lead role in tracking the situation.

What was it? A disease that just 13 months earlier had blipped on the CDC's radar screen was rapidly turning epidemic, particularly among gay men and drug addicts. Yet no one agreed on what to call it. Because the disease critically weakened the immune system and was often accompanied by a rare cancer, it had been labeled gay-related immune deficiency, or GRID, by some people, gay cancer by others.

The novel disease wasn't, however, restricted to gays. At the meeting, a less exclusive name was suggested: acquired immunodeficiency syndrome, or AIDS. The acronym had staying power—as has the epidemic. More than 22 million people worldwide have died of AIDS over the past two decades, and today 42 million others live with the virus that causes it. New medicines have made it possible for those who have the disease to lead productive lives, but there is still no cure.

—*By Unmesh Kher*

ON THE MARCH
A 1983 rally called for more funding for AIDS research

July 27, 1982

Bedeviling an Empire

What TIME Said Then

So it was that the Right Rev. Ronald Reagan journeyed last week to the holy precincts of the 41st annual convention of the National Association of Evangelicals. His fiery sermon mixed statecraft and religion. He made politicians from Moscow to Washington sore... —*March 21, 1983*

Ronald Reagan had carefully prepared for the moment, rewriting by hand several portions of the speech. An earlier draft read, "Surely historians will see [that the Soviets] are the focus of evil in the modern world." But speaking before the National Association of Evangelicals in Orlando, Fla., Reagan made the speech tougher by removing the business about the historians. He also denounced calls for a nuclear freeze, saying that to agree to one would be to accede to "the aggressive impulses of an evil empire." The President's uncompromising rhetoric unsettled members of the Washington establishment, who warned that it would reheat the arms race and might threaten peaceful coexistence with the Soviets.

But Reagan managed to touch the hearts and minds of those who mattered: the rebels behind the Iron Curtain who ultimately brought it down. Nathan Sharansky read Reagan's speech in a cell in Siberia. Knocking on walls and talking through toilets, he spread the word to other prisoners in the Gulag. "The dissidents were ecstatic," Sharansky wrote. "Finally, the leader of the free world had spoken the truth—a truth that burned inside the heart of each and every one of us."

—By Romesh Ratnesar

STEADFAST He was not an intellectual (one critic called him an "amiable dunce") but Reagan stuck to his core beliefs

March 8, 1983

PEOPLE POWER:
The new Soviet leader
meets Bulgarians in
Sofia, October 1985

March 11, 1985

Taking Charge: My First Day on the Job

Most important things in my life happened in March: I was born in March. I joined the Communist Party in March. It was in March 1990 that I was elected President of the U.S.S.R. And it was in March 1985 that the Politburo nominated me General Secretary of the Communist Party.

An urgent phone call had reached me the evening before. I recall it was Sunday, because on a weekday I would never have been home earlier than 10 p.m. The caller told me that Konstantin Chernenko, the General Secretary of the party and leader of the Soviet Union, was dead.

His predecessor and my mentor, Yuri Andropov, had told me before he himself got seriously ill that I must be prepared to assume the highest responsibility one day. I knew what he meant. He tried to ensure that event. In December 1983, two months before his death, Andropov sent a written message to the Central Committee plenum, suggesting that "Gorbachev should be entrusted with actual leadership." I did not know that he did this. And neither did the plenum. In 1988, I learned that Chernenko had simply cut off that part of the message and concealed it. And so he became General Secretary. If Chernenko did not exist, the Old Guard would have invented him.

Still, with Chernenko so feeble and ill, it was I who had to preside over the Politburo sessions throughout most of his tenure. Thus it fell to me to convene the emergency session at his death. I called Foreign Minister Andrei Gromyko, one of the longest-serving and most influential members of the Politburo, and arranged to meet him privately half an hour before the session. I told Gromyko: "Too many problems have piled up in the country. I believe you and I have to tackle them together." Gromyko answered: "I fully agree with your appraisal of the situation." His support was most crucial.

I came back home at about 3:30 a.m. My wife Raisa met me at the door. Too worked up to go to bed, I suggested that we take a stroll. Those paths near our dacha in Zhukovka, they witnessed so much. "We've never talked about this," I said. "But I must tell you now: I might become one of the candidates. You know, I've tried to quit politics thrice. But it has become the cause of my life. If they do nominate me, I can't shirk it. The people have been watching for too long, watching their leaders passing away one by one. If we offer them another one like that, we should all be fired. Is our generation a generation of cowards? Things in the country are grave; problems are enormous. It's hardly a coveted job under the circumstances. But my conscience tells me I must do it."

Raisa listened in silence and then answered, "As always, I rely on you."

I really knew the shape the country was in. I saw the mess around me. But I still entertained illusions that the system could be reformed. I had tried a mini-*perestroika* during the 10 years I was in charge of Stavropol, in southern Russia. But the curbs imposed from above had not let us go farther. So, I thought, it's at the top that we must start changes to let the people breathe. But even after I got there, the system fought back, resisting and biting. Nothing changed in the country at large. The party officialdom defended its power. Only in 1988 did I realize that the totalitarian communist system could not be reformed. It had to be dismantled and replaced by democracy. Yegor Ligachev, a hard-line Politburo member, said at a later point, "It was only too late that we discerned a social democrat in Gorbachev." Indeed, it was. I strove for peaceful changes; I did not want any boot stomping. They did stomp their boots in 1991 with their failed coup d'état—and I left. Still, I dragged them to the point of no return. There could be no going back to the past and to the old system.

—*By Mikhail Gorbachev, As told to TIME's Yuri Zarakhovich*

Gorbachev led the Soviet Union from March 1985 until its demise in late December 1991.

Take a Pill and Make Your Day

Fluoxetine hydrochloride had been approved for use in Belgium the year before. But the imprimatur of the U.S. Food and Drug Administration heralded a whole new era. At first, only scientists were excited, because Prozac, as the Eli Lilly company christened it for the market, was the first in a new class of medications that would treat depression by exquisitely controlling the levels of serotonin, a brain chemical involved in mood. But the FDA's approval letter became the founding charter for a Prozac nation, as vast numbers of U.S. consumers were seduced by a prescription to lift one's mood. Today they spend more than $1 billion on Prozac each year, to treat not just depression but also obsessive-compulsive disorder and premenstrual syndrome. The cultural revolution has escalated with the arrival of new antidepressants without Prozac's occasional side effects—nightmares, violence, loss of libido. And in the tradition of imitation as the ultimate form of flattery, by 2001 cheaper, generic fluoxetine hit the market.   —**By Alice Park**

Dec. 29, 1987

What TIME Said Then

Introduced in January 1988 and hailed as safer than competing medications, Prozac quickly surged to star status, thanks to skillful promotion by manufacturer Eli Lilly, glowing word of mouth among doctors and patients, and heavy media attention. — *July 30, 1990*

THE HEIR:
Bin Laden
with Afghan
supporters
in the '80s

SIPA

Terror Gets A New Boss

The explosion was so powerful it was heard several miles away, and its reverberations would eventually travel around the globe. The car was nearing its destination, the al-Falah Mosque in the Pakistani frontier city of Peshawar, when it hit the land mine. All four passengers in the vehicle—a father with his two young sons and another youth—were killed.

Chief among the dead that Friday was Sheik Abdullah Azzam, 48. It was the second attempt on his life. Earlier in 1989 a bomb was planted beneath the pulpit of a mosque where he was supposed to preach and pray, but the bomb did not explode. Azzam, a Palestinian, had become the most prominent advocate of a jihad to save the Muslim lands from infidel encroachment. Thanks in part to his writings and diatribes, Islamic fighters from around the world traveled to Afghanistan to defeat the Soviet Union.

Azzam's killers have never been identified. But the man who gained the most from his demise was his deputy, Osama bin Laden, who took over the role of first among the *jihadis.* The Saudi aristocrat had been the chief financier of Azzam's organization and a devoted follower since the early 1980s, when he came under Azzam's influence while studying at Jeddah University. Disagreement between master and protégé over the shape of a post-Soviet Afghanistan led to a parting of ways in early 1989, and soon bin Laden went off to found al-Qaeda. With Azzam dead, bin Laden assumed ideological seniority in the movement. He would expand the struggle from Muslim territory deep into the heart of the West itself.

—*By Ghulam Hasnain*

The Hated Wall Is Smashed

What shall I do? Order you to shoot?" As a crowd of 20,000 of his countrymen implored him to "Open the gate!" on that chaotic Thursday evening, Harald Jäger, head of passport control at the Berlin Wall's Bornholmer Strasse checkpoint, kept shouting that rhetorical question at the guards under his command. It was nearly 11 p.m., four hours since Jäger heard the stunning news on TV: the East German Politburo, responding to weeks of peaceful demonstrations and a flood of refugees fleeing through Hungary and Czechoslovakia, had announced that all citizens could leave East Germany at any crossing "immediately."

Suddenly Jäger, 48, held in his hands the fate of thousands of people—as well as that of the Wall he had so faithfully watched over for all 28 years of its existence. His orders were to turn the protesters back unless they had proper documents, but he knew that attempting to do so would result in bloodshed. So, as recounted in *The Wall: The People's Story*, shortly after 11 p.m. Jäger told his men at the gates to "open them all." By dawn, an estimated 100,000 delirious East Ger-

CEMENTING ENMITY
Building the barrier,
August 1961

Nov. 9, 1989

**THE FALL: Water
cannons didn't stop
Berliners from
destroying the Wall**

■ What Goes Up ...

The Berlin Wall fell amid dramatic scenes of exaltation and reunion, witnessed by a global television audience. But its building was furtive, hurried and surprisingly underpublicized. It would take years of escapes, failed attempts at escape and visits by U.S. presidents and other leaders to make the Wall the most prominent symbol of a world divided between superpowers.

According to a 1986 article by Timothy Ryback in the *Atlantic* magazine, the first shadowy visions of a wall dividing occupied Berlin were entertained by the Western powers rather than by the Soviets. As Ryback tells it, in early December 1956, following the bloody Hungarian revolution, NATO leaders met in Paris. West Germany's Foreign Minister sketched a scenario in which East Germans might rise up against their government, and West Germans might cross the border to aid them—igniting a major war. The solution: divide the city by a wall. U.S. officials backed the plan, Rbyack says, but the radical idea was never implemented. Applying similar logic, the Soviets erected the Wall five years later, at a moment of great cold war tension following a June summit meeting between U.S. President John F. Kennedy and Soviet leader Nikita Khrushchev in Vienna.

mans had slipped past him on their way to a raucous celebration in West Berlin.

Over the next few days, the revelers hammered away at the most notorious symbol of Soviet communist repression and toasted their newfound freedom with bottles of champagne. But joy was soon dampened by the daunting burden of rebuilding the backward East. More than a decade after Germany officially unified in 1990, the country is still suffering the hangover.

—*By Daniel Eisenberg*

What TIME Said Then

What happened in Berlin last week was a combination of the fall of the Bastille and a New Year's Eve blowout, of revolution and celebration ... West Berliners pulled East Berliners to the top of the barrier along which in years past many an East German had been shot while trying to escape; at times, the Wall almost disappeared beneath waves of humanity. —*Nov. 20, 1989*

DENIS PAQUIN—REUTERS—CORBIS

**RONALD REAGAN AND
MIKHAIL GORBACHEV**
Just after shaking hands in a
19th-century villa on Lake
Geneva on Nov. 19, 1985,
the two leaders decided to
talk privately in the villa's
pool house. The informal
chat stretched into almost an
hour of joshing camaraderie
and sometimes heated
discussion. The best news:
the two emerged smiling

PA-WIDE WORLD

Fateful Meetings

**DONALD
RUMSFELD
AND SADDAM
HUSSEIN**
The enemy of my
enemy is my friend.
So went the thinking
at the Reagan White
House, as the U.S.
began tilting toward
Baghdad in its three-
year-old war with Iran.
On Dec. 20, 1983,
special envoy
Rumsfeld met Saddam
and delivered a
personal note from
Reagan expressing
U.S. good will

GETTY IMAGES

**PRINCE CHARLES
AND DIANA SPENCER**
Lady Sarah Spencer, Diana's
sister, would later say she
was "playing Cupid" when she
invited the Prince of Wales to
her family's Althorp estate for
a shooting weekend in
November 1977. She may
have been joking, for she had
designs on Charles herself.
The future princess was not
overly impressed: "What a
sad man," she thought

Snapshots

■ Bill Gates

The son of a prominent Seattle lawyer, Gates has spent most of his life around computers. He initially encountered them as a seventh-grader in 1967, when the proceeds from a mothers' club rummage sale were used to buy a machine for Seattle's Lakeside School. Gates soon devised a class-scheduling program so that he could take courses with the prettiest girls. *—April 16, 1984*

■ Lee Iacocca

Friends say he does not have the patience for politics, and he concurs. "If you only talk cars, people say you're a provincial son of a bitch. If you're outspoken, then they say you're running for office." *—March 21, 1983*

■ Carl Sagan

For all his extracurricular interests, Sagan was a highly productive researcher. As always, he was iconoclastic. Although most astronomers were studying the more distant realms of the stars and galaxies, Sagan opted for the nearby planets under the tutelage of the late Gerard Kuiper. He realized that planets were the most likely places for extraterrestrial life to be found in his lifetime. He also anticipated that the U.S. would soon embark on an ambitious program of planetary exploration. At a party just before Sputnik 1 spurred American space activity, Sagan made a perspicacious wager: he bet a case of chocolate bars that the U.S. would reach the moon by 1970. He won with five months to spare. *—Oct. 20, 1980*

■ Donald Trump

Something about his combination of blue-eyed swagger and success has caught the public fancy and made him in many ways a symbol of an acquisitive and mercenary age. Now that a new year has dawned, observers of the Trump empire can rather easily imagine some of the emperor's resolutions for 1989: to make more money than ever, to buy more expensive gewgaws than ever, to get more publicity than ever—and if Mikhail Gorbachev passed up a chance to visit Trump Tower during his visit to New York last month, well, there's always next time. *—Jan. 16, 1989*

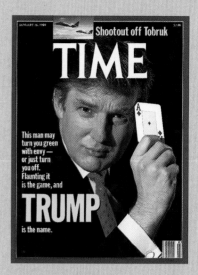

■ Lech Walesa

Shortly before 5 o'clock, the dignitaries were introduced. Poland's President Henryk Jablonski, a silver-haired figure in a black overcoat: a smattering of applause. Franciszek Cardinal Macharski of Cracow wearing crimson biretta and robes: hearty applause. Then Union Leader Lech Walesa, the improbable hero of last summer's strikes, bundled in his customary duffel coat: tumultuous applause. After a moment of silence, Walesa lit a memorial flame, which at once burned brightly despite a light drizzle. Said he: "This monument was erected for those who were killed, as an admonition to those in power. It embodies the right of human beings to their dignity, to order and to justice." *—Dec. 29, 1980*

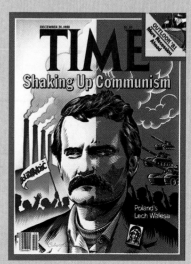

JAN 1, 2000 What a party! From Sydney to Paris to New York City, revelers hailed the millennium as one. Three years later, French and American citizens were bitterly divided over a new war with Iraq

1990s

When the U.S. and a surprising band of allies rolled back Iraq's invasion of Kuwait, and the Internet wove us together in a dazzling digital Web, it seemed a new world order was at hand. But after the Big Bang of the millennium, a stalemated election and devastating terrorist attacks dashed our visions of a brave new world

JULY 7, 1990 Tenors of the times—Placido Domingo, José Carreras and Luciano Pavarotti—bring opera to the masses in their first appearance, at the Baths of Caracalla in Rome

SEPT. 15, 2000 Bizarre, outsized theatrical effects! Aging athletes! Crocodile Dundee! One hundred fifty tap dancers! Aboriginal shamans! It could only be the opening of the Olympic Games, this time Down Under in Sydney

2000

Spinning a Web To Span a Globe

Nobody was paying attention to Tim Berners-Lee and his pet idea. He was a young British scientist at CERN, a high-energy physics lab in Geneva, and he had a radical new way for scientists to share data by linking documents to one another over the Internet. He had kicked around a few different names for it, including the "Infomesh" and the "Information Mine." But he wasn't getting much interest from his bosses. His proposal came back with the words "vague but exciting" written across the cover.

So Berners-Lee took his invention to the people. He posted a message to a newsgroup—a kind of electronic public-access bulletin board—announcing the existence of the "WorldWideWeb (WWW) project." The message included instructions on how to download the very first Web browser, also called WorldWideWeb, from the very first website, *http://info.cern.ch.* Berners-Lee's computer faithfully logged the exact second the site was launched: 2:56:20 p.m., Aug. 6, 1991.

He posted it, and we came. From that day forward traffic to *info.cern.ch* rose exponentially, from 10 hits a day to 100 to 1,000 and beyond. Berners-Lee had no idea that he had fired the first shot in a revolution that would bring us home pages, search engines, Beanie Baby auctions and the dotcom bust, but he knew that something special had happened. "Of all the browsers people wrote," Berners-Lee recalled, "and all the servers they put up, very few of them were done because a manager asked for them. They were done because somebody read one of these newsgroup messages and got that twinkle in their eye." **—By Lev Grossman**

Aug. 6, 1991

PIONEER: Berners-Lee with an early Web page

At Long Last, Freedom

When the slender, white-haired Nelson Mandela, then 71, first glimpsed the crowd assembled at the gates of Victor Verster prison, he instinctively raised his right arm in the black-power salute of a clenched fist—a simple public gesture that he had not been able to make during his 27 years, six months and

Feb. 11, 1990

seven days of imprisonment. His release had been orchestrated by South Africa's white minority government, but it was a reluctant acknowledgement of what had become an unstoppable force. The world had lost patience with white rule in South Africa and had placed its faith in a man whom no one had seen in decades. The man who emerged was unbowed but also unsophisticated about modern media. (On that first day, he thought a furry TV boom mike was a weapon.)

Mandela knew that he had to banish any public bitterness to win racial reconciliation in his divided land. During what he called his "long, lonely, wasted years" in prison, he never doubted his country would achieve democracy. It just took a lot longer than he had expected.   **—By Richard Stengel**

Stengel collaborated with Mandela on his 1994 autobiography, Long Walk to Freedom.

A Foreshadowing of Terror's Reach

STUNNED
Rescuers help a victim after the explosion in the World Trade Center garage

Feb. 26, 1993

ALAN TANNENBAUM—POLARIS

The bomb went off shortly after noon and shook the building like an earthquake. Our offices on the top floors of 1 World Trade Center (the north tower) went dark. No one knew what had happened, but within minutes the emergency lights kicked on and our 700 employees at Cantor Fitzgerald calmly headed for the stairs.

The stairway quickly became a traffic jam as 20,000 workers on lower floors were also evacuating that cold February day, but the Cantor folks didn't panic. Some of them lashed their ties and belts to the wheelchairs of handicapped people and carried them down the 105 flights of stairs. Others helped those who were unable to walk unaided down to the 25th floor where fire fighters, who were on their way up to help, took over. We all made it out.

As we look back now on the 1993 attack, in which six people were killed and more than a thousand were injured when a terrorist bomb exploded in an unoccupied van in the Trade Center's underground garage, it's clear that for many of us the event was a false ceiling on the limits of terror. We thought at the time the attack was a warning to be prepared. And so, Cantor Fitzgerald and the other tenants and building managers of the World Trade Center tried to prepare. We took what we thought were exhaustive efforts to safeguard ourselves from any future incidents. Security at ground level and below was tightened. Stairways were rebuilt to make it easier for police and fire fighters to enter. Many businesses, including ours, worked on detailed disaster-recovery plans in the event we lost our buildings. And then life went on. Somewhere in the consciousness of those of us who worked in the Trade Center was the belief that terrorists, like lightning, would not strike the same place twice.

When it did, on Sept. 11, our preparations were not in vain. The added measures no doubt saved the lives of thousands of people who evacuated safely. Yet to a tragic extent, we had erected defenses against the past. We could not have foreseen the horror and destruction that Cantor Fitzgerald, New York City and our nation would experience. We lost more than anyone could have imagined.

In the months following Sept. 11, our employees committed to rebuilding with a new purpose: to care for the families of the 658 victims we lost. We announced on Sept. 19, 2001, that we would distribute a quarter of our company's profits to these families for a period of five years, and cover 10 years of health care. We can never regain what was taken from us that day, but we keep the memory of our friends in our hearts and their families by our side.

—*By Howard Lutnick*

Lutnick is chairman and CEO of investment firm Cantor Fitzgerald.

Oct. 3, 1995

SPLIT DECISION
Watching the verdict
at Augustana College,
above; Simpson and his
team getting the news

Color Us Divided on O.J.'s Innocence

What Americans had in common that day was that we stopped using the phone for a few minutes: according to AT&T, phone traffic dropped 60% from 10 a.m. to 10:05 a.m. P.T. In appliance stores and offices and diners, we dropped everything and watched as nine blacks, two whites and one Hispanic rendered their verdict: Orenthal James Simpson was not guilty of the murder of his ex-wife Nicole Brown Simpson and her friend Ronald Goldman.

On the streets of African-American neighborhoods and the campuses of black colleges, we high-fived total strangers in jubilation. In white communities, we sat in quiet shock or vocal dis-

gust. On radio shows, we hailed the acquittal of the black former football hero as payback for years of police racism, and we condemned the decision as a simple case of money buying freedom. At New York City's Rikers Island prison, we broke into applause, guards and inmates alike. In the Harriet Tubman battered women's shelter in Minneapolis, Minn., we cried.

Later that day, on the TV news, we watched each other watching, and soon that watching became the bigger news, for it taught us what else we had in common. We, each of us, could not believe that the other side could feel the way it did. We realized that we were not, in fact, "we."

—By James Poniewozik

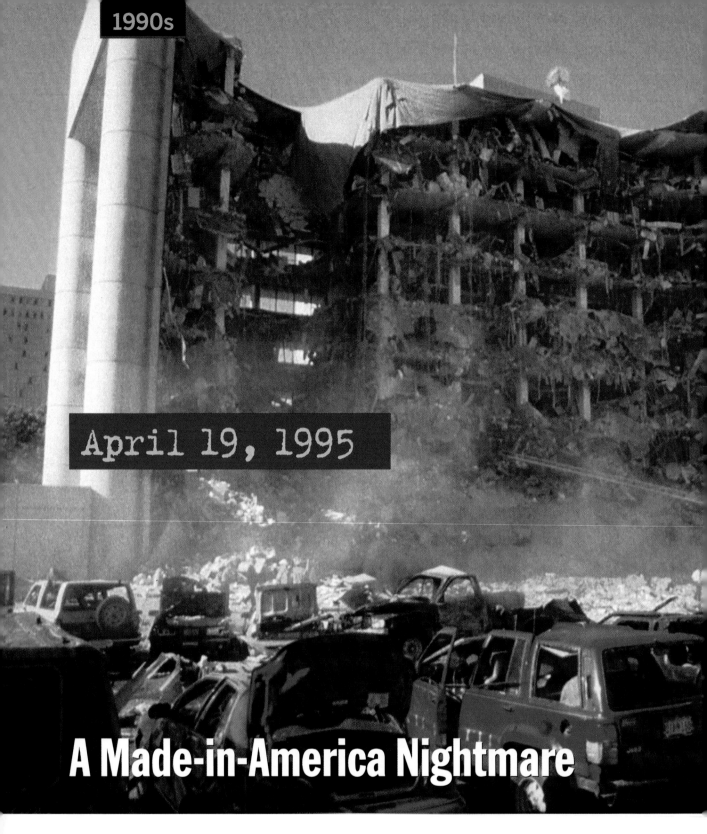

April 19, 1995

A Made-in-America Nightmare

N o one noticed the smoke seeping from the windows of the rental truck as Timothy McVeigh pulled up to the Alfred P. Murrah Federal Building that gray morning. McVeigh had lit two fuses to the 7,000-lb. fertilizer bomb in the truck and then parked it beside the building's day-care center. The explosion vaporized the front of the building, leaving a yawning cross-section of oozing cable and smoke. The dead would number 168,

including 19 children. (At least six people who survived or lost loved ones in the bombing have since killed themselves.) When McVeigh was executed in 2001, the former Gulf War soldier remained convinced that his deadly deed had punished the U.S. government for its 1993 siege of the Branch Davidian compound near Waco, Texas.

For America, the bombing was an introduction to mass-casualty terrorism. The enemy was no longer uniformed pla-

REFLECTIONS: The main memorial is sunk beneath ground level, silencing sounds of the city

DEVASTATED: The remains of the Murrah building in Oklahoma City

■ Honoring the Fallen

As Americans contemplate creating a memorial to the grief caused by the 9/11/01 attack on the World Trade Center, two touchstones are most frequently cited: the Vietnam Memorial in Washington, designed by Maya Lin in 1981, and the Oklahoma City memorial commemorating the 1995 bombing of the Alfred P. Murrah Federal Building.

Designed by Hans and Torrey Butzer, Americans then living in Berlin, the Oklahoma memorial was dedicated on the fifth anniversary of the tragedy. The three-acre site consists of two portals, inscribed with the numerals 9:01 and 9:03: the attack occurred in the space between, at 9:02 a.m. A long reflecting pool spans the portals, and a field of 168 chairs occupies the footprint of the building. The bronze chairs are mounted on blocks of glass, and each is inscribed with the name of a victim of the bombing. A section of the ruined wall of the building remains standing.

The Vietnam and Oklahoma City memorials share an important element: each takes care to honor each of those fallen by name.

toons but lone extremists in our midst. They could not be easily ferreted out—or understood. But Oklahoma City also wrote the book on recovery. The survivors have become indispensable companions for the families of 9/11 victims. And the memorial to the homegrown tragedy shows that traumatized cities can unite, as author Edward Linenthal puts it, "to protest the anonymity of mass death."`

—By Amanda Ripley

What TIME Said Then

Glass fell like sharp rain over whole sections of the city. Toys were scattered everywhere, haphazardly mingled with arms and legs, the remnants of a destroyed day-care center on the second floor. It was as if some immense, wicked child had ransacked her nursery and dismembered her dolls.
—*May 1, 1995*

What the investment banks had valued a
few weeks ago at a modest $14 was soaring
to $30 ... $45 ... $55 and into the wild
blue-chip yonder. Finally, as stunned
brokers sat with phones glued to ears, the
opening price was reached: $71 a share.
—*August 21, 1995*

Netscape's IPO Sparks a Boom

We didn't know what it was. We
had never opened a browser.
We had never gone on the Net.
But we had heard that the deal
would be hot, so we at Cramer
& Co., my $250 million hedge fund, duti-
fully put in for our share of stock in the ini-
tial public offering of Netscape. We got several thousand shares. And we, along with
most everyone who got some, made an ab-
solute killing. The stock, which we thought
was going to be priced at $12 a share, came in
at $28 and then opened at $71. (It peaked
at $97.62 on March 17, 1999.) We were gid-
dy. We had never made money that quickly in our lives. We thought it was going to
be a one-time event, never to be repeated.

Looking back now, we recognize that
Netscape was simply the blueprint, the un-
choreographed start of what would become the greatest bull-market show in history. Taken to market by Frank Quattrone,
the now fallen investment banker who
would turn Silicon Valley greener than irri-
gation made the San Joaquin; nurtured by
analyst Mary Meeker at Morgan Stanley,
who would later admit that she was "trying
to value companies without any historical
valuation tools or rules"; and overfed by
hyped-up traders who could buy stock online using their Netscape browser, this deal
changed everything. We began to classify
every company as new economy vs. old
economy, and the chorus of bankers, analysts
and traders would embrace the new despite its unproved nature, inability to gen-
erate profits and lack of operating history.

Forces coalesced to create the greatest
bubble in history. Valuations, earnings and
common sense were sacrificed on the altar
of instant IPO riches. If Netscape worked,
the next 100 Netlike deals could work, and

NETSCAPE

Aug. 9, 1995

the next 200, because the online economy
would have to supplant the off-line economy.
Dotcom alchemy had begun. Trillions of
dollars in losses later, we now know what hit
us: a mania that eventually destroyed the
bull market itself. The banker perpetrators
are now being pursued by the authorities,
the analyst anointers held in low esteem.

And what became of Netscape? It got
swallowed up by AOL, under which it lost
most of its already dwindling market share
to Microsoft—and now operates primarily
as a Web portal, one of the legions fighting
for eyeballs and Internet dollars.

—*By James Cramer*

*Cramer watches markets for TheStreet.com
and is co-host of CNBC's Kudlow & Cramer*

BROWSERS
**Netscape's Marc
Andreessen, seated
at right, and his
team of techies**

The Last Hours of a Princess

They had finished an intimate dinner at the Ritz Hotel, and Dodi Fayed, an Egyptian-born multimillionaire, and Britain's Princess Diana were on their way to his opulent 10-room apartment overlooking the Champs-Elysées. But the couple never made it to Fayed's place. At 12:23 a.m. the speeding Mercedes in which Diana, 36, and Fayed, 41, were riding crashed into the 13th pillar of the Alma tunnel on the right bank of the Seine River. Fayed and the intoxicated driver died at the scene. Diana was declared dead at 4 a.m. at Paris' Pitié-Salpetrière Hospital.

Acres of flowers, cards and teddy bears quickly began piling up outside Diana's home at Kensington Palace. But the outpouring of grief seemed to catch the royal family off guard, and it took almost a week before Queen Elizabeth II finally declared her admiration for her erstwhile daughter-in-law. Yet Diana had left an indelible mark on the Windsor clan. In the days, weeks and years since, the once staid monarchy has continued to strive for that common touch that made Diana the people's princess. —*By Anita Hamilton*

Aug. 31, 1997

GRIEF: Stunned Britons filled London's streets to view the funeral cortege; inset, Diana leaves the Ritz

PATRICK DURANT—CORBIS SYGMA

AP/WIDE WORLD

**BLUE FORMULA
A small pill with
stirring results**

March 27, 1998

A Potent Breakthrough

Like the reliable erection its new product promised, Pfizer's stock had risen 21% in the previous two months. Some urologists bought rubber stamps so they could churn out prescriptions, and equally excited patients booked advance appointments.

Despite all that, Viagra, the world's most popular prescription party drug, didn't get much of a party the day the FDA gave its much-anticipated O.K. to the new wonder drug, sildenafil citrate. That's because giant pharmaceutical companies— even ones that have a license from the government to print money in blue-pill form— aren't really party places. "We had a nice dinner that night," admits Dr. Ian Osterloh, who oversaw the development of the impotence treatment.

The drug, originally designed to treat angina (patients still had angina, but some also noted a different kind of agitation they had not had in some time), was approved as expected on the final day of the FDA's six-month priority review. News of the approval immediately went up on the FDA website, the first time the agency notified the public of its decision in real time. And then the world celebrated: *Cocoon* was played out in every Florida retirement community, marriages moved on to deeper problems, the pornography industry was democratized, and talk-show hosts enjoyed a new way to tell Bill Clinton jokes.

—*By Joel Stein*

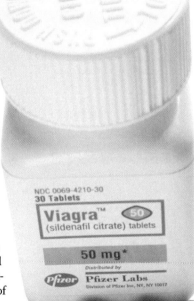

KARIE HAMILTON—CORBIS SYGMA

"UFFICIENT SCALE FARMS OT OGRESS"

JUST SAY N

DEM LIC Y

"GLOBALONEY!"
Masked activists
protest in Seattle

Nov. 29, 1999

A Call to Arms for World Trade Dissenters

I spent that Tuesday in Seattle with 50,000 of my closest friends, some wearing turtle costumes, some wearing gas masks, some carrying union banners, and everybody chanting "They say free trade; we say fair trade" and "Hey hey, ho ho, WTO has got to go." To almost everyone's surprise, we managed to shut down the World Trade Organization's Seattle conference and sent the WTO's leadership hightailing it back to Geneva without what it came for: an agreement for a new round of closed-door negotiations on global trade rules. An expert at a progressive think tank in Washington described it as "a kick in the groin of the ruling class."

I believe the cops started the real violence, however. Early in the day, when the delegates couldn't get to the convention center through the ring of activists, the police sprayed gas and shot rubber bullets at people engaging in civil disobedience by linking themselves together with pipes and locks. That was the first violence, although the media focused more on young white guys in black ski masks who broke store windows later in the day. While I disapprove in principle of property destruction, I've often wondered whether we would have got as much press as we did without the Starbucks trashing.

I had been in Seattle on and off for nine months, helping organize this mobilization on behalf of the advocacy group

Public Citizen, with a coalition of unions, environmental groups, faith-based and human-rights networks, family farmers and consumers. We knew this confrontation between civil society and corporate rule was going to be exciting when we went to the Ruckus Society's direct-action camp in September and learned how to scale overpasses, hang banners and get busted. We knew it was going to be big when we joined the AFL-CIO in planning sessions to mobilize workers from all over the U.S., and when local politicians participated in our critique of so-called free trade.

For the organizers of the protest, the experience was an epiphany: none of us could remember a time when such divergent organizing traditions blended so seamlessly in a single action. The legacy of that week is felt today in the movement against war in Iraq and manifest in groups like the Alliance for Sustainable Jobs and the Environment, an exemplar of "blue-green" solidarity forged that day. The legitimate expectations of working families and the imperatives of sustainable development are now a part of the conversation about the direction of U.S. policy in an increasingly globalized economy. 　　　　　　　　　 **—By Mike Dolan**

Dolan is an organizer for Public Citizen's Global Trade Watch.

EYEBALLING A MESS:
A Florida ballot
examiner checks for
hanging chads

■ A Farewell to Chads?

In the wake of the presidential election
fiasco of 2000, Americans across a
broad swath of the political spectrum
called for electoral reform. But it was not
until late October 2002—only a week
before the midterm elections—that
Congress passed and President Bush
finally signed into law a reform bill,
dubbed the Help America Vote Act.

The law provides states with $3.9
billion to replace punch-card and lever
voting machines with new equipment,
help provide better access for voters with
disabilities and accommodate voters for
whom English is not their first language.
Other funds will be devoted to recruiting
and retaining poll workers and targeting
high school and college students as
potential poll workers.

Unwilling to wait for reform at the
federal level, legislatures in 11 states
passed voting-reform measures by the
2002 elections. Among them was
Florida, ground zero for the vote-
counting problems of 2000. But Florida
officials were embarrassed to encounter
major problems in counting the ballots in
the party primary elections in September
2002. Electoral reform, it seems, may
be easier to vote for than to achieve.

Dec. 12, 2000

EARTHSHAKING:
The rivals meet on
Dec. 19 to put the
bitterly contested
race behind them

The Court Rules, and Bush Wins

At about 10 o'clock on the night the U.S. Supreme Court handed down the 5-to-4 decision that put him in the White House, George W. Bush was already in bed, keeping his usual early hours. In Virginia, his top political adviser, Karl Rove, was also in pajamas, monitoring the cable news channels. Hearing the news on one station, he raced to phone the Governor's mansion. "It's over," Rove said. "Congratulations, Mr. President."

Bush turned on his TV. After 35 days of court reversals, hanging chads and false endings, the Texas Governor wasn't ready to start receiving salutes. "What are you talking about?" he said. Analysts on CNN seemed to be saying Al Gore still had a chance. "I'm not hearing the same thing you're hearing," Bush said. "I tell you what I'm going to do. I'm going to call a lawyer."

Bush dialed Jim Baker, his father's Secretary of State, who was leading the recount battle in Florida. But even the seasoned lawyer couldn't provide a quick answer. The Supreme Court opinion could be fully understood only by reading the back pages of the filing. When Bush called, just the first pages had dribbled out of the fax machine. After agonizing moments, Baker got the full ruling and confirmed that George W. Bush would indeed become America's 43rd President. —*By John F. Dickerson*

AP/WIDE WORLD (2)

What TIME Said Then

You could almost see ... the regret and relief and resolve when Bush rose last Wednesday night with tears in his eyes and promised, "I will work to earn your respect," all but admitting it just does not come with the job when you win this way. —*Dec. 25, 2000*

The Day al-Qaeda Attacked America

Phillip Godfrey was thrown into a wall on the 55th floor of 1 World Trade Center when the first plane hit. A seminar on the logistics of trade with Mexico had just begun, and it was Godfrey's job as a Benchmark Hospitality employee to help set up. Now Godfrey, 43, asked Jesus not to let the floor give way. When it steadied, he focused his attention on getting everyone out. Like many of those at the Trade Center that morning whose names we never heard—people who weren't fire fighters or cops—Godfrey thought of others first. He heard the women who worked with him screaming, and he ran to them. "It will be all right," he

soothed, uncertain whether it was true but finding no choice but to believe it.

A 20-year Trade Center employee, Godfrey had survived the 1993 bombing, and knew it would be best to leave immediately, even though he also knew that official procedure called for staying put. Now calmer, the women said they had to get their bags. Godfrey thought about grabbing his own bag, which contained a ring with his initials and the gold onyx watch that needed cleaning, but he didn't. Instead, he asked whether anyone had searched the meeting rooms. No one had, so Godfrey ran to clear them while the others started

Sept. 11, 2001

■ From the Ashes

In late February 2003, after a closely watched competition, a design for the future of the former World Trade Center site was selected. The winning plan was created by Daniel Libeskind, 56, a Polish-born American architect. The symbolic center of the site, 30 ft. deep, will be sections of the "bathtub," the scorched pit in which the foundations of the two towers once stood. A museum in Libeskind's signature angular style will anchor the site. On three surrounding sides an ensemble of towers will rise, including a 70-story office structure with a spire that rises to the patriotic altitude of 1,776 ft.— the world's tallest building. It's a grand plan—but competing interests at the site, plus a weak economy, may delay its construction for years.

downstairs. A frightened co-worker wanted to wait for the required phone call to evacuate. Godfrey, who looked out the window and saw hell, said, "Trust me, the person on the other end of that phone—they're not there." Godfrey nearly had to carry the man out.

After Sept. 11, strange things happened to Godfrey. Hailed as a hero, he lost his job when Benchmark started layoffs. People said he did amazing things that he didn't do: hoist a woman down the stairs, give someone a $50 bill to get home. Instead, he did the simple work of a man who has learned that, as he says, "we need each other." **—By John Cloud**

What TIME Said Then

If you want to humble an empire it makes sense to maim its cathedrals ... The Twin Towers of the World Trade Center ... and the Pentagon ... are the sanctuaries of money and power that our enemies may imagine define us. But that assumes our faith rests on what we can buy and build, and that has never been America's true God. *—Special Issue, September, 2001*

SINGLED OUT:
Bush cited
Mohammad
Khatami's Iran,
Saddam
Hussein's Iraq
and Kim Jong
II 's North
Korea as
threats to
world peace

Jan. 29, 2002

In Terror's Wake, the Enemy Is Defined

I n late December 2001, chief presidential speech-writer Mike Gerson made a simple request whose repercussions would be felt around the world. "Here's an assignment," he told his colleague David Frum. "Can you sum up in a sentence or two our best case for going after Iraq?" President Bush had yet to decide to target Saddam Hussein, but he was moving in that direction and wanted a rationale for overthrowing Saddam in his State of the Union address. As Frum wrote later in his book, *The Right Man*, "I was to provide a justification for a war."

Frum needed to explain why Saddam, even if he wasn't involved in 9/11, should be a target in the war on terror. What linked Saddam with Islamic terrorist groups, Frum thought, was their hatred of Western democracy.

In that way, they were similar to the Axis powers of World War II. In his memo to Gerson, Frum called Iraq part of "an axis of hatred," but Iraq was the only member of the group singled out at that point.

Frum never expected his stern language to pass the President's lips. But as new drafts of the address were written, it stayed in the speech. It was Gerson who injected theology into the key phrase, turning "hatred" into "evil." By mid-January, Bush had decided that Saddam had to go. Other countries were added to the axis—first Iran, then North Korea. In the address, Bush declared, "States like these constitute an axis of evil, arming to threaten the peace of the world." Frum's simple assignment had given birth to the defining phrase of a presidency. —*By James Carney*

MONICA LEWINSKY AND BILL CLINTON The President and his intern had met each other before Nov. 15, 1995, but it was on this night—during a government shutdown—that she flashed him the straps of her thong at a birthday party for a staff member. Clinton later asked her to join him alone. The rest, sadly, is history

Fateful Meetings

POPE JOHN PAUL II AND FIDEL CASTRO At their first meeting, Nov. 19, 1996 at the Vatican, the communist leader invited the Pope to visit Cuba. John Paul agreed; in January 1998, he arrived for a five-day stay, right, and was given a hero's reception

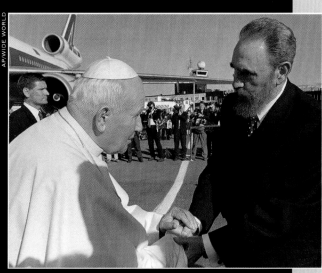

COURTNEY LOVE AND KURT COBAIN Backstage at Portland's Satyricon nightclub, Cobain caught Love's eye on Jan. 12, 1990. Nirvana's lead singer thought she looked like punk heroine Nancy Spungen; she told him he looked like Soul Asylum's lead singer. Feigning anger, Cobain grabbed Love playfully and wrestled her to the ground. "There was beer on the floor," Love recalled. Above, the family in 1993

Snapshots

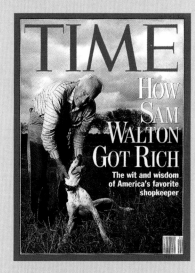

TIME

HOW SAM WALTON GOT RICH

The wit and wisdom of America's favorite shopkeeper

■ **Sam Walton**
"I'm not sure I ever figured out this celebrity business. Why in the world would I get an invitation to Elizabeth Taylor's wedding? And I still can't believe it was news that I get my hair cut at the barbershop in Bentonville. Where else would I get it cut? Why do I drive a pickup truck? What am I supposed to haul my dogs around in, a Rolls-Royce?" —*June 15, 1992*

POLICE UNDER FIRE

TIME

BORIS YELTSIN, the bad boy of Soviet politics, battles Gorbachev in a crucial vote this week

Russia's Maverick

■ **Boris Yeltsin**
At 6 ft. 4 in., Boris Yeltsin looms over listeners and lecterns, taming audiences of 1 to 100,000. His ramrod-stiff stance, his thick silver hair, his deep, slow voice all suggest a coil of powerful but slow-burning energy. Yet when he starts to speak the effect is not intimidating but mesmerizing, even entertaining. —*March 25, 1991*